It's
Been An
Exciting Ride!

It's
Been An
Exciting Ride!

Jack Echlin's Story Of Echlin Inc.

As told to Christopher Gilson

Foreward

Over the 10 years before his death on April 26, 1988, Jack Echlin and I were close friends. The warmth of that friendship is something forever to be cherished.

Jack, another wonderful friend, Jim Bolan, and I were a frequent luncheon trio at a Florida club. Often we would talk about Echlin.

Here was a gracious, modest man whose inventive mind, perseverance, and dedication to excellence had built, from the smallest of beginnings, a proud, thriving enterprise. In doing so, he had made important contributions to the progress of one of the world's great industries.

As one who long has been and still is in the public relations profession, I found continuous fascination in hearing, bit by bit, what added up to a remarkable story.

It was a story Jack's wife Beryl, his successor as chairman Fred Mancheski, Jim Bolan and I, and many others had urged him to write. But, though he might agree at the time that it would be a good idea, it was something easy to put off doing.

Then one day early in March of 1988, Jack was confronted with little choice in the matter. We were having a pleasant visit, and I pulled a note pad from my pocket.

"Today, Jack," I said, "we're going to begin the Echlin story. You do the telling. I'll do the writing. You do the editing. Between us, we'll produce a manuscript."

The response was that combination of engaging smile and little chuckle so much associated with Jack Echlin. The writing of the story did begin that day.

We worked on it over the ensuing weeks until I had to go north on business in April. Sorrowfully, the day before I left was the last time I saw my good friend.

A great part of the story had been completed, however, and we had discussed what yet was to go into it. To Beryl, their daughter Jane, their son John, Fred Mancheski, and many helpful individuals at Echlin goes deep gratitude for added content of which I know Jack would have approved.

Christopher Gilson

Table of Contents

John E. Echlin 1897-1988

Images

"To see Echlin today!

What an exciting ride we've had, how unbelievably far we've traveled! What an incredible journey it's been, how bright the horizons are ahead!

Here is a publicly held corporation with well over $1,250,000,000 a year in sales and close to that figure in assets. A business with a host of quality products and the finest of distributors handling those products. A company with more than 14,000 employees in operations that stretch across the United States, extend into Canada and Mexico, reach down into South America, and span the seas into Europe, South Africa, and Australia.

When I view where Echlin is today and look into the future at its impressive outlook for continuous growth, images of memorable yesterdays flash across my mind . . ."

The Early Years

Chapter 1
The Early Years

How It All Began

How well I remember December of 1915!

As a 19-year-old wireless operator aboard ships sailing out of San Francisco, I was in port for a few days. My 23-year-old brother Earl had an automobile repair shop at 2410 California Street in the Fillmore District, and I dropped by to see him.

The building was a 24-foot storefront that went back 70 feet. Although Earl had started the business only three months before, the wooden structure was cluttered with cars on which he and one helper were working. The two of them were so busy, usually under cars, that Earl had no time to collect bills due him. He asked whether I might like to try my hand at it.

The bills weren't that difficult to collect, and on each return to the shop, I found myself developing a fascination for automobiles. Earl, pleased with the results of the bill collecting, noticed this. He suggested I might like to quit my job as a wireless operator and come into the business with him. I had had the same thought!

What had been Earl C. Echlin became Echlin and Echlin.

With Growth, More Space

My job was to continue with the bill collecting, solicit new business as repairs were completed on cars in the shop, and when I wasn't doing either of these, work on cars myself.

Things went along in good order. But when America entered World War I, Earl decided to enlist. It was agreed that I would stay and operate the business while he was overseas.

The need for car repairs expanded during the war. Our business was brisk, so much so that it was outgrowing the little shop. It was necessary to move to larger quarters, and I found a suitable brick building at 2255 Bush Street. It had been occupied by the telephone company.

Various alterations were required to meet our particular needs. The Anglo California Bank, with which we were doing business, made a loan to the owner to do this work and rent the building to us. The location proved ideal for our purposes.

But fate has its way of sometimes confronting one with setbacks. It was no time to be ill, yet I got what then was known as the Spanish influenza. What a jolt this was! I had borrowed money from the bank to finance our expanding business, and naturally had incurred other obligations. By the time I recovered from the illness, I was broke, owing more than our total assets represented!

Perhaps fate has its reasons. The struggle to pay all creditors and get the business liquid again may have been preparation for struggles to come.

At any rate, once solvency had been regained, it was time to move ahead.

Additions

Car repair is an essential business and a good business. But one can get tired of just repairing automobiles, especially if there are other things that can be done with cars at the same time, such as selling them.

While retaining the repair operations, we added the selling of used cars. The two went well together.

And, of course, there were still more things that could be done with automobiles. Trucks were needed in San Francisco. We found a way to help provide them.

Our method was to buy new Model T Fords, remove the bodies, and in their place attach what was known as a Ralston extension. We sold them equipped in this manner, enabling buyers to put on the types of truck bodies they required for their hauling.

Simultaneously, we bought used Model Ts, overhauled them, took off the bodies, and replaced them with those we had removed from the new Fords. These gave buyers what amounted to virtually new cars.

Equipping the trucks with four-speed transmissions became another part of the business. This was accomplished with a device that had a low and high gear by means of the conventional type of gear shifting. In conjunction with the low and high gears built into Model Ts, trucks were given four speeds forward and two backward; in other words, a low low and a high high forward. We often referred to it as a Lo Lo, Hi Hi, Lo Hi, Hi Lo transmission.

With these several activities, the business grew. By the time Earl returned from France, it had made a little money.

Getting Prepared

With good prospects for expanding our production activities in the growing automotive industry, it was obvious to me that I should know much more than I did about engineering. While I had acquired some knowledge in working with cars and trucks, there was a great deal I needed to learn about the technical aspects of manufacturing.

Consequently, I enrolled in a two-year night course at the Polytechnic School of Engineering in Oakland. This schooling was to prove invaluable down through the years in our striving for constant improvement in our products, developing new products, and continuously adding to our production facilities.

At the school, another young man and I became good friends. His name was Elmer Lillie. Elmer later was to join our company and become an important part of our organization, remaining with us until he retired in 1964.

Not long after completing the engineering course, I decided it also would be a good idea to have some knowledge about law. I could visualize contract negotiations, liability coverage, and all sorts of situations in which it would be beneficial to know some legal basics.

This led to my enrolling in a correspondence course to study law. I found this extremely valuable. What I was able to learn from it has been advantageous many, many times since.

The First Product

Our entry into true manufacturing and merchandising came through a headlight we devised to improve the safety of driving at night.

In those days, headlights were merely spotlights with plain glass at the fronts. Considering that many roads were still primitive, and most of them abundant with curves in rural areas, these ordinary lights provided only some degree of frontal vision and none to the sides.

We called our invention the SAFE-LITE. It was an auxiliary headlight at the center, pivotally mounted on a bracket fastened to the radiator filler spout that cars had in those days.

The light turned in the direction the car was being steered. This was achieved by using a Bowden wire. A Bowden wire was the assembly of an outside, or casing, wound in such a way that it formed a flexible tube. A hard steel wire was inserted inside the tube. This, connected to the front axle and tie rod, moved in and out in response to the steering direction of the car. The SAFE-LITE was separately wired to a switch convenient to the driver for turning the beam on and off.

At the same time, we perfected a lens that actually spread light over the road area. With this, the SAFE-LITE not only focused light on curves, but increased frontal vision.

To market the product, we established the Safelite

Manufacturing Company and sold through distributors. But we couldn't have picked a worse place than California with its stringent spotlight laws!

SAFE-LITE was not a spotlight. A spotlight is a concentrated beam within control of the driver, who can turn it at will on anything he or she wishes. SAFE-LITE, on the other hand, was not directly within the driver's control. It turned only in the direction the car was steered and spread light horizontally. But try to convince the California police!

Fortunately, spotlight laws in some of the other states were not so rigid and police not so stubborn about understanding the distinction! And South America! What a market that turned out to be! No spotlight laws, lots of winding roads. Overall, then, despite California, its birthplace and manufacturing site, SAFE-LITE did well.

Another Move

As our repair business and machining operations grew, it was necessary to farm out work to a number of machine shops. One was Schnerr & Scheeline at the corner of Golden Gate Avenue and Gough Street in San Francisco.

Edwin S. Scheeline, who was also engaged in another business, had decided to withdraw from the firm, and its name was changed to J.J. Schnerr Company. Mr. Scheeline had taken promissory notes for $63,000 for the purchase of his interest. Not able to collect the money, he filed suit and won. But in order to collect, he had to take over the business. He did not want to operate it himself and asked us to join him.

J.J. Schnerr, using a Bear Brand trademark from the grizzly bear in the California flag, produced piston rings, pistons, piston pins, and flywheel ring gears for sale to parts jobbers. In addition, the company manufactured spiral ring and pinion gears of higher and lower ratio than stock equipment, as well as transmission gears and shafts for Fageol trucks. Fageol, prominent in trucks at the time, later became part of American Car and Foundry, now ACF, Inc.

In our discussions, Mr. Scheeline advised Earl and me that the Schnerr company had no liquid assets. He also revealed that sales were running at a rate of $36,000 a year, far short of a break-even point standing at $120,000 a year.

Nevertheless, we consulted with the Anglo bank on the whole matter, including the bleak financial picture. We were assured that we could borrow needed money and were encouraged to go ahead.

Thus, in 1924, we moved from the Bush Street building to the Schnerr location.

One of the Wonders!

Obviously, some drastic action had to be taken to get things in order at Schnerr.

It took all the liquid assets of SAFE-LITE to handle the cost of our consolidation and to meet the back payroll. We needed more money.

The Anglo bank lived up to its word. With no visible means of paying it back, we were granted a $20,000 loan. I'll never know why. Mrs. Dorothy B. Pardo, my longtime secretary and a devoted and valuable part of our company, made this comment in something she later wrote, "Why they ever lent us the money is one of the seven great mysteries of United States commerce!"

We quickly abandoned the piston and piston pin business because it was totally unprofitable. Although the flywheel ring gears were produced by a primitive method, we expanded their sales to parts jobbers up and down the Pacific Coast and in other areas. We continued to make gears for Fageol. And, thanks in great part to South America, we turned out a steady flow of SAFE-LITEs.

One thing was clear, however. In order to reach a break-even point of $120,000 a year, we had to find other products to manufacture. Moreover, they had to be items we could produce without prohibitive investment and executive and engineering attention.

Something To Celebrate

We also found we had to overcome a bad reputation that had developed around the J.J. Schnerr Company.

This we managed to do by reincorporating in Nevada under the name of Echlin & Echlin, Inc. Why Nevada? California laws were a bit peculiar. We felt that more flexible ones, such as those in New Jersey and our neighboring state of Nevada, would be more to our advantage as we sought new opportunities.

With one salesman in the field, we did begin to build a little more volume. This came from expanding the flywheel ring gear sales and production; also from making oil-pump gears for oil burners manufactured in San Francisco.

Then, in 1925, came the kind of chance for which we had been searching. It was with the Millwood-Simmons Company, a small firm that distributed electrical parts to jobbers in the 11 western states. We made a deal to provide oil-pump and igniter gears for Millwood-Simmons to handle through its network of jobbers.

This was a break we badly needed. Moving our production above the $120,000-a-year mark called for a well-earned, though mild, celebration. Things were looking good!

Variety and Choice

Who knows when America's love affair with the automobile began?

It well could have been during those mid-1920s when such a variety of cars, many of them beautiful by today's or any other day's standards, glistened in the showrooms and drew admiring eyes on the roads. To think back and list just some of the names so familiar then is to observe, with no small regret and much nostalgia, how few have survived:

Apperson	Hudson
Auburn	Hupmobile
Autocar	Locomobile
Brush	Marmon
Buick	Nash
Cadillac	Oldsmobile
Chalmers	Overland
Chandler	Packard
Chevrolet	Paige
Chrysler	Pierce Arrow
Dodge	Stanley Steamer
Duesenberg	Studebaker
Durant	Stutz
Essex	White Steamer
Ford	Willys
Franklin	Winton

It was a great time to be in a business associated with automobiles. We had our own love affair with them. We were above the $120,000-a-year mark. Our business was growing. What could have been a rosier outlook for two young fellows looking to the future?

But fate was lurking around the corner again!

The Unexpected!

Selling to Millwood-Simmons went well for about a year. Then a problem hit us!

The Millwood-Simmons people were having a hard time collecting for merchandise they sold, including our gears, and started going broke! Our only option was to take over the oil-pump and igniter gears from them and sell to jobbers ourselves.

So, we assumed their inventory of these items in full settlement of the money they owed us. This left us with thousands of dollars in trade acceptances, the equivalent of promissory notes, that had been discounted at the bank.

Talk about a tight financial situation! We had taken over the Schnerr company, which had no liquid assets. We had borrowed $20,000 with no visible means of paying it back. And while we had managed to retire part of that loan, assuming the Millwood-Simmons trade acceptances took us far above the credit limit our bank had set.

Let it be said that the cooperation and generous attitude of Louis Sutter, Anglo's chief loan officer, are remembered to this day with the utmost gratitude. I recall so well that in this instance Louis wasn't sure he had the authority to extend us as much as we needed. But he didn't want to say no.

He handled it by taking me in to meet Herbert Fleishhacker, president of the bank and a leading figure in San Francisco. Mr. Fleishhacker asked me a few friendly questions, smiled graciously, and said we could have the money. Louis Sutter was pleased. I was relieved and delighted!

Looking Eastward

Our first marketing step after acquiring the Millwood-Simmons inventory was to send our salesman, Tony Ruegg, on a trip throughout the East to try to get jobber accounts beyond the western states. He didn't fare too well.

What's more, sales volume from the Millwood-Simmons jobbers was falling off. Many were returning the merchandise they had purchased instead of paying their accounts. There was no way we could meet payrolls and other expenses with gears rather than dollars!

There was an encouraging development, however, in our effort to get into the eastern market. We obtained distribution through Brown & Green Ignition Sales Company of New York, later to become Kem Manufacturing Company. The initial orders were significantly large.

Meanwhile, we also had succeeded in getting business from Chevrolet and Durant to supply oil-pump and igniter gears for their Pacific Coast manufacturing. But win some, lose some. We had lost the Fageol business because they had sold out to ACF and moved to Cleveland.

On the whole, we were holding our own. There had been

setbacks. There had been forward strides. We were learning that the key was to keep the latter ahead of the former.

Where We Stood

As things shaped up by the end of 1926, our product line consisted of igniter gears, water-pump shafts and impellers, and flywheel ring gears.

We had found it prudent to phase out SAFE-LITE. Other states were adopting stricter spotlight laws, and we were having a harder time persuading them that ours was not a spotlight. We felt we could not go it with the South American business alone. We were reluctant to give up what had been our first product. It had served us well, but the time had come to part.

Our gears were manufactured under the trademark of "Bear Brand Gears." We had retained what J.J. Schnerr adopted from the grizzly bear in the California flag. Our emphasis was on quality and on being capable of supplying a range of needs.

In this regard, a statement in the foreword of a 12-page catalogue we published in 1926 is pertinent:

"We manufacture and carry the most complete line of igniter and oil-pump gears obtainable in the United States . . . If the gear you want is not listed, send in the old gear to us with the name, year, and model of the car. The chances are we can furnish the gear."

How large were we when we made that bold claim?

Well, three women comprised our office force—a bookkeeper, a stenographer, and a billing clerk. Out on the factory floor there weren't many more employees than that. We certainly weren't impressive in numbers, but we were in the quality of products coming out of that small plant.

Quality. It's an overused word. It often is a misused word. The fact is, though, that from the days of the little repair shop at 2410 California Street in San Francisco, it has been fundamental to Echlin's growth.

The Upward Climb

Chapter 2
The Upward Climb

An Art in Itself

February 8, 1927, stands as the most memorable date of all.
It was the day Beryl Goldsworthy and I were married in San
Francisco.

We had met eight months before. There had been no
question in my mind from the very beginning that Beryl was
going to be my wife. It was simply a matter of persuading
her. In the process of doing so, I'm sure she received the
longest love letter on record.

Beryl was born in Grass Valley above San Francisco. At
one point in the courtship she was leaving for a visit with
relatives there. I told her I would write her a long letter. It
was long all right, written in ink along the center of an entire
roll of adding machine paper. And at frequent intervals, I
inserted the number 88.

Why 88? In the international telegraph code, as Beryl knew
from conversations about my days as a shipboard telegraph
operator, 88 means love. It took some doing for her to read
that letter, but the repeated message certainly was clear.
And the feeling it conveyed has not changed for an instant
over all the years since. What a wonderful and helpful part
of my life she has been, how fortunate I have been to have
her!

That same year, thanks to what was learned from a man
by the name of Frank Beckman, Echlin entered a period of
solid growth.

We continued to be disappointed in the jobber aspect of our business. As brought out earlier, we had obtained distribution through Brown & Green Ignition Sales Company of New York. Initial orders had been highly encouraging, then began to fall off. This, coupled with the inability of our salesmen to build business with jobbers, led me to try my own hand at selling.

What I quickly learned from that experience was how little, if anything at all, I knew about selling!

That's where Frank Beckman entered the picture. Frank was associated with Beckman-Hollister Company, a sales and business consulting firm in San Francisco. I heard of a night course he was giving in salesmanship. Since my first efforts at selling had ended in what had to be regarded as total failure, it was obvious I was a prime candidate for anything that would teach me something about it. So, I enrolled in the course.

One of the first things to become clear in listening to Frank was that selling is an art in itself. There is so much more to it than appears on the surface that it has been the subject of untold numbers of books. I even wrote one myself later. When I realized there was an art to using one's knowledge about a product to create in another a desire and need for that product, and when I absorbed Frank's insights into applying this, things changed.

Learning to sell proved to be a pivotal development for Echlin's future.

What a Difference!

It was an exhilarating experience to apply my new-found techniques and discover that they were effective! It actually was no task to sell oil-pump and igniter gears to jobbers— the better jobbers, at that, who were able to pay their bills.

This turned out to be only part of it, though. The jobbers were buying, but their ability to sell the gears to the trade left much to be desired. This, of course, was due in part to our not being very high on their priority lists. Their primary interest was in selling such large-volume items as piston rings, spark plugs, brake lining, and accessories.

We tried to get them to let us do missionary work with their salesmen and train them in selling our products. But they wouldn't give us any time for this. Nor were they receptive to allowing us time at their sales meetings.

An idea struck me! Why not organize a one-evening sales talk, based on Frank Beckman's course, to teach jobber salesmen how to sell *all* the products they handled, but use our oil-pump and igniter gears to illustrate how sales could be made? It worked!

Wildfire Describes It!

The first talk was given to the San Francisco sales organization of Chanslor & Lyons. By that company's own admission, this did more to improve the efficiency of their salesmen than anything they previously had attempted. In no time, they wanted the same talk given to all their stores along the Pacific Coast from Canada to Mexico.

Not only that, Chanslor & Lyon spread the word to their jobber friends, including Colyear Motor Sales Company. The more talks, the more jobbers there were buying and successfully selling our gears: such respected and well-financed firms as Henderson Brothers, Patterson Parts Company, and Gilfillan Brothers, the first replacement manufacturer of ignition parts. We really were moving ahead now!

From that time on, as we built our own sales organization, the technique used in those talks served as the underpinning.

The Grand Tour

The year 1928 was a milestone for the company. Business was expanding as a result of the one-evening sales courses for the jobber salesmen. Earl concentrated on production to assure a flow of quality products to meet the rising demand for them. My main responsibilities were on the sales and marketing side to keep the demand rising.

In April, then, Beryl and I embarked on a nationwide trip by automobile to make calls on existing outlets and to develop new ones. What an expedition it was—almost four months and some 13,000 miles!

Our car was a Studebaker sedan. We had to be sure that all the luggage would fit into the trunk because the back seat and floor were crammed with catalogues, sales materials, samples, and everything else needed to show and promote our wares.

Our itinerary took us south to Los Angeles. From there, we traveled the southern route to Texas, then to Oklahoma City, Kansas City, St. Louis, and Chicago. Next, following the approximate route of the New York Central Railroad, we went on to New York, with numerous stops along the way. From New York, there were side trips, including Boston. Heading westward, we paralleled the Pennsylvania Railroad route across Pennsylvania to Pittsburgh, Columbus, Indianapolis, and Chicago again. Then, we went up to Minneapolis and St. Paul and down to Sioux City and Omaha. On from there, we crossed Colorado to Denver, headed to Salt Lake City, and finally returned to San Francisco.

Talk about seeing the country! Many of the roads were still a bit rugged in those days. And, of course, the car wasn't air-conditioned. Beryl would wait for me as I made calls. That could be pretty warm as the weeks moved from late spring to summer. Sometimes, when we knew my calls would be somewhat lengthy, Beryl would go browsing in stores or watch a movie in an air-conditioned theater to keep out of the heat.

Four months of constant traveling—roads, stops, unpacking, packing, hotel beds, restaurant meals—can make home look better than ever. We were delighted to be back. But we were buoyed by what had occurred. We had met wonderful people who became lifelong friends and associates. Important gains had been achieved for our company. And we had enjoyed ourselves.

A Long Relationship Begins

Things can happen in strange ways!

By a fortunate turn of events, a decision to join the National Standard Parts Association (NSPA) and exhibit at its annual show led to our becoming affiliated with the National Automotive Parts Association (NAPA). This was an historical development for our company.

The NSPA show was to be held in Cleveland that fall of 1928. While we were preparing our exhibit for it, Russ Fleisher, San Francisco manager for Colyear Motor Sales, one of our major customers, suggested that NAPA would be an excellent outlet for our oil-pump and igniter gears.

This idea appealed to us immediately. In Dallas, on our trip, I had been invited by Jack Heffelfinger, manager of the NAPA warehouse there, to give my talk. The superiority of the facility and the way it was operated impressed me deeply. It was far above the general run of other warehouses and jobbers.

It is important to understand that the automotive replacement industry was still largely in its infancy at that time. Many of the jobbers were offshoots of wrecking houses or machine shops. They were not well experienced in business management and merchandising. Collecting from them was often slow, sometimes unreliable. Thus, although we recognized how valuable they had been in enabling us to build business, the thought of distributing through NAPA was extremely attractive.

It so happened that NAPA's annual meeting was to be held in Detroit at the same time as NSPA's meeting and show in Cleveland. Russ Fleisher told me that he and C.C. Colyear were going to the NAPA meeting.

I'll never forget Russ for his suggestion that if I could arrange to be on the same train with them, it would be a great opportunity to gain Mr. Colyear's support for our becoming designated as an exclusive supplier of oil-pump and igniter gears for NAPA outlets. As a director himself, Mr.

Colyear could be instrumental in lining up support from the other directors.

Naturally, I arranged to take the same train. Mr. Colyear and I became friendly. He offered to arrange an interview for me with the NAPA directors at the Detroit meeting. There was no doubt about my being pleased to accept.

Enter the surreptitious!

There was a great rivalry between NSPA and NAPA, mostly on the former's part. Because of this, I had to perform a bit of a cloak-and-dagger act.

NSPA had a policy of paying the travel fare and all other expenses of exhibitors attending its meeting and show. The only way my attendance could be verified was to be on hand to check in and check out.

This required my going to the NAPA meeting in Detroit without the NSPA people in Cleveland knowing I was doing so. It was accomplished by flying to Detroit to meet with the NAPA directors at an appointed time, presenting my line, having it approved and adopted, and returning to the NSPA meeting in Cleveland in time to check out.

A vanishing-reappearing performance; a happy outcome!

A Dramatic Surge

In approving and adopting our gear line, the NAPA directors talked in terms of quantities we considered to be too optimistic. But they backed up what they had said. Orders immediately began arriving in quantities approaching those they had discussed. We had to go to three work shifts a day to turn out the volume of gears being ordered.

As far as we knew, the volume we attained exceeded that of any other gear manufacturer in the industry—in terms of gears, not dollars.

For a small company. our sales were high. Moreover, our profits were excellent. NAPA warehouses paid their bills promptly, in many cases before they even received the merchandise. We were in a period of prosperity we never had known before.

Our affiliation with NAPA indeed was historic for our company. To this day, it has been a continuous, harmonious relationship of immense benefit to us. Over the years, many warm, valued friendships have come from it.

From the very outset, there was Henry Lansdale, for example. As general manager of the organization, Henry contributed so much to NAPA's becoming the great force it is in our industry. Our business dealings soon extended into a close and lasting personal friendship. His son Ben, a University of Michigan electrical engineering graduate, later joined Echlin, bringing important skills to us.

In those early years, too, a wonderful friendship developed with Carlyle Fraser. Carlyle, along with Wilton Looney who succeeded him in 1961, built a jobbing business in Atlanta into the magnificent Genuine Parts enterprise we know today. As a treasured friend, as our major customer, and along the line as a director and large stockholder in our company, Carlyle always will be remembered with the highest affection and esteem.

Broadening the Base

Late that same year, our company entered into negotiations to buy the ignition business Gilfillan Brothers, located in Los Angeles, had operated successfully for a number of years.

They were going out of the business because of several patent suits against them. They had reached a settlement with Delco-Remy and Auto-Lite. They agreed to discontinue ignition production. The patents under which they were being sued had expired, however, and we were free to go into the ignition business even though Gilfillan could not continue in it.

In part, we were motivated by the realization that car manufacturers were redesigning gears to last longer. We foresaw in this the possibility that at some time in the future demand for our oil-pump and igniter gears might decline.

It made sense to have a hedge against this. The Gilfillan operation would give us one.

Prelude to October

Though the stock market crash in October signaled the beginning of the Great Depression and dark times ahead, 1929 was an important year for Echlin from a long-term standpoint.

Purchase of the Gilfillan ignition line was consummated in January. All of a sudden our small company had to learn a new type of business, hire more people, and make the transition to a considerably larger sphere of endeavor.

One step was to employ John D. Leslie, formerly sales manager in the Gilfillan Kansas City branch. Johnny quickly made a major contribution by compiling our first ignition catalogue.

For this catalogue, our company developed an entirely new format. Up to that time, the general policy in the industry was to show contacts, condensers, and caps and rotors in separate tables. This necessitated going from one table to another to look at them. Our innovation was to show all parts on one line to fit any model, making it possible to get the information much more quickly and easily.

When the catalogue was published in July, it immediately attracted a great deal of attention. And it was a big sales booster by enabling the user to offer related parts. This new format soon was copied by all others in the industry.

Another Gilfillan man, N.H. Bertram, was retained to represent us in the East. In other areas, we affiliated with manufacturers' agents to handle our ignition line.

While all this was occurring, our gear business was expanding rapidly as orders poured in from NAPA warehouses across the country.

Now we really could see bright vistas ahead. But along came October. By year's end, we faced heavy obligations amid the great uncertainty of what lay before us in a plunging economy! Yet, in terms of products and distribution facilities, the year had brought us solid advances in the right direction.

To come back briefly to our first catalogue and others we issued during those early years. . . . An interesting bit of information turned up more than half a century later.

On a visit to Japan in 1987, Scott Greer, group vice president for our operations in the Southern Hemisphere, met a Mr. Yamaguchi. This gentleman owns an automotive parts manufacturing business which he started in Japan shortly after World War II.

Mr. Yamaguchi told Scott about the first catalogue his company had prepared, and showed him one that had been used as a guide in putting it together.

What do you think he handed Scott? It was an early catalogue from Echlin.

We didn't know how far our influence had spread!

Weathering The Storm

Chapter 3
Weathering The Storm

Finances Again!

As the Depression began deepening early in 1930, we were short of funds again. As well as we were doing with the gear business through our affiliation with NAPA, the Gilfillan purchase had taken much of our capital.

This confronted us with a problem! Gray & Danielson, a San Francisco company, had been molding our ignition parts. A devastating fire wiped out the company. We had to move quickly to fill the void that was created.

The logical thing for us was to have our own molding equipment rather than to continue to farm out the work. But we didn't have the capital this required.

A solution appeared. A.E. Podesta, then foreman in the factory and later superintendent of factory operations, offered to put up $20,000 to help finance the purchase and installation of our own molding equipment. In order to take advantage of the offer, we had to amend our articles of incorporation to permit the company to enter into a partnership.

This done, we formed a partnership between Echlin & Echlin, Inc. and Adolph Podesta called Universal Molding Company. This, in effect a subsidiary of Echlin & Echlin, was established at our Golden Gate Avenue and Gough Street quarters. We furnished our part of the investment by transferring to Universal Molding Company our ownership of the molds for producing the ignition parts.

Universal Molding proved to be a valuable investment for both the company and A.E. Podesta.

Other Developments

Although we ended the year with a net loss, we counted our blessings for surviving 1930 when so many other firms were going under because of the Depression.

Especially noteworthy were several things on the plus side.

For one, our younger brother Victor joined the company as a salesman and proved to be an excellent one.

For another, NAPA approved us as the supplier of ignition parts for its outlets across the country.

A third was the opening of a warehouse in Cleveland, Ohio. We had been warehousing merchandise in Chicago under the supervision of a manufacturer's agent. This had not been wholly satisfactory, and we elected to establish our own. The warehouse, located at 1220 West Ninth Street in Cleveland, enabled us to stock merchandise for shipment to eastern NAPA warehouses. Hugh Bauerlein, who came with us earlier that year, was named manager and did an outstanding job.

Another significant step was the appointment of Ernest W. Lenz of New York City as our export manager to handle Echlin products, along with others he already represented, for distribution to countries outside of North America. Ernie remained in this capacity for many years, and shares much of the credit for the company's expansion into foreign markets.

All in all, then, though we operated at a loss, actions taken in 1930 produced important future benefits for the company.

Continued Pursuit

With the Depression gaining momentum, 1931 brought its portion of adversity. At the same time, there were some bright sides.

The year began with an amusing occurrence.

John R. Scott, formerly with Sherman, Clay and Company, the leading Pacific Coast music supply house, wanted to try his hand at selling our products. We liked him, gave him the chance, and assigned him to the Atlantic Seaboard territory, working out of our Cleveland warehouse.

When we advised Hugh Bauerlein of this, he was concerned. He expressed it this way in a letter dated March 3, 1931:

"I sincerely hope that Mr. Scott is the type of man who can talk to such men as Mr. Baxter, Mr. Zismer, Mr. Martin, and Mr. Locke . . ." All of these men were important to us as customers.

Hugh had no need to worry. Scotty became an outstanding salesman and made many lasting contributions to our company. He left us in 1939 to become president of the corporation that owned the NAPA warehouse in New York, but continued as a close family friend and staunch supporter of Echlin.

In August of that year, we had to give some bad news to all of our employees whose salaries were more than $100 a month: a pay cut. We had been able to hold our own pretty well. We had excellent outlets for our products. In many ways, we were moving forward from the standpoint of having a solid operation. But the Depression was making its impact.

It was during this year also that Delco-Remy and Electric Auto-Lite Company instituted patent infringement lawsuits against all manufacturers of ignition replacement parts.

Adding Products

Optimism, hope, and tenacity were three needed qualities during those dark Depression days. We had them. We kept telling ourselves it couldn't go on forever and made plans and took steps accordingly.

With the sound network of outlets that had been developed, a logical move was to add products to our line.

In 1932, we came out with our first ignition coils. There was a highly favorable reaction to them from our customers. We were confident about their future.

That year we also signed a royalty contract with Irven E. Coffey and Stephen E. Gandalfo to manufacture and sell an invention Mr. Coffey had patented. This was a device for testing ignition coils. It was a thermo-sensitive piece of metal that measured the heat of the spark produced by the ignition coil. We merchandised it as the "Thermo-watt Meter."

Meanwhile, the patent infringement lawsuits Delco-Remy and Electric Auto-Lite Company had filed began heating up.

We joined with seven of the other leading manufacturers of ignition replacement parts in establishing a fund to defend ourselves against the suits. We and one other company did retain our own law firms, however, because we were not satisfied with the one the group had selected.

These suits weren't the only ones with which we had to contend. P.R. Mallory and Company of Indianapolis sued our company, alleging that we were infringing on their patent for attaching tungsten directly to the ignition contact arm.

Actually, we were not infringing. We had developed our own method of brazing, rather than riveting, tungsten directly to the arm. Rivets made them heavier, increasing inertia in an opening direction so that they would not close in time. Brazing eliminated this problem, and we were the first in the industry to do it.

Even so, as we got into the suit it appeared that the best way out was to reach some form of compromise. We did this by agreeing to pay P.R. Mallory and Company a small minimum royalty.

For the Nation, a New Era

The election of Franklin D. Roosevelt brought hope to the country that it would climb out of the Depression's ravages.

It also brought the strong hand of government into our lives and into our workplaces.

In August of 1933, I was asked to attend a meeting of the new National Recovery Administration (NRA) in Detroit. The purpose was to write a code of ethics for our industry. Members of the National Standard Parts Association had attempted to have one passed that would have been disastrous for NAPA. This had been fought successfully, and the objective now was to come up with a suitable alternative.

At the Detroit meeting we did produce one that would have been satisfactory, had it been adopted. But it wasn't printed before NRA was declared unconstitutional in 1935, hence was abandoned.

That Detroit meeting is vivid in my memory because of something that happened while I was away and was told upon returning. It was the death of our dear friend and colleague, Edwin S. Scheeline, then secretary-treasurer of our company. His coming to us those years back with a proposal to join him in the J.J. Schnerr Company had changed the course of our lives and our business. He had been a wonderful associate and we were going to miss him. Mrs. Mae Scheeline was elected to take his place.

Two years later, Mrs. Scheeline and her son Edwin Jr. were elected directors of the company. At this same time, Edwin was elected treasurer, while his mother remained as secretary.

As 1933 moved to a close, there was a new feeling in the nation. President Roosevelt had taken some firm actions. Government was moving in directions it never had taken before, and there was considerable concern, particularly in the business community, about those directions. But the national outlook seemed to be brightening.

In our case, with new products added to our existing lines, we were able to continue to expand in the mid-1930s. But there were changes.

Realignments

In 1935, my brother Earl, whose little auto repair shop had been the start of it all two decades before, passed away. Earl had been seriously ill for some time. It had been difficult for him to continue directing our factory operations which he had done so capably. His passing was a great loss to us. To him belongs a great amount of the credit for the long distance our company had traveled in those 20 years during which he played such an important and pivotal role.

Earl's place on our board was taken by Victor Echlin who, from the time he came with us in 1930, had done an outstanding job in sales.

Ben Lansdale, mentioned earlier, who had been one of our eastern representatives, was called to the factory to take charge of plant operations.

It was in 1935 also that Robert L. Bradford came to us with a device he called a motorstat. We were preparing to enter the test equipment business at the time. It was an excellent vehicle for this, far superior to anything on the market, and we entered into a royalty agreement with him that gave us exclusive manufacturing rights. At the same time, since he needed money, we gave him part-time employment.

Although Bradford brought us a good product, he also brought us much grief in years to come.

Another thing that should be recorded about 1935—and it surely was on the plus side—was the conclusion of the patent litigation that had been brought against the other manufacturers and us by Delco-Remy and Electric Auto-Lite Company in 1931. We were completely vindicated. What a relief it was not to have this hanging over our heads any longer!

Too, the nation indeed had emerged from the Depression. While it was far from booming, the economy, with much of what then was called pump priming by the government, was moving forward.

Echlin had weathered the storm.

Decisive Years, Major Moves

Chapter 4
Decisive Years, Major Moves

Further Growth

The years between 1936 and 1940 were especially meaningful for Echlin.

It was plain that if we were to continue to expand our product lines and sales, we would need larger quarters. We were outgrowing the space we had occupied from the J.J. Schnerr days. It was becoming increasingly difficult to operate under conditions that were getting more and more cramped.

But moving to the kind of space we needed, and which we envisioned we would require to accommodate growing volume, meant substantial outlays of capital. It was capital we didn't have. Staying afloat during the Depression and continuously adding products had placed heavy demands on income.

The answer was to raise some money by selling stock in the company.

Our first step in doing so was to reincorporate as a stock company under the laws of the State of California. At the same time, we changed the company's name from Echlin & Echlin, Inc. to Echlin Manufacturing Company, in order to connote more clearly the nature of the business.

Two types of stock were issued. One was six percent preferred with a par value of $10.00. The other was common with a par value of $1.00. Through sale of both types of shares, we were able to raise several thousand dollars and could now look for a suitable larger location.

A desirable piece of property was purchased in the fall of 1936. It was a lot at the corner of 16th and Vermont Streets in the Potrero District of San Francisco. We immediately set to work designing a three-story, 36,000 square-foot building to house our factory and administrative offices.

The building was completed in March of 1937 at a cost of approximately $72,000. It had a frontage of 100 feet on 16th Street and extended 140 feet back on Vermont Street. We began moving our factory equipment into it as soon as the construction was finished, and moved our offices there on April 7. Now we were much better situated to proceed with growth.

Out in the Territories

The year 1936 also marked the beginning of NAPA regional conferences to build closer contact and rapport with dealers in their own territories. The first was held in Kansas City, then it was on to the Pacific Coast, back to the Midwest, east to New York, with the final one in Atlanta. I had the opportunity of making the complete tour.

Those regional meetings, which were continued, proved of great value in building friendships with people in the field. It would be difficult to count how many of the conferences I have attended since that first year. Every one of them has been enjoyable and beneficial.

Too, what was called the Moto-Lab came to the height of its popularity in 1936. It consisted of giving demonstrations and conducting educational meetings on motor tune-up for garagemen and electrical specialists. We had two men, the Pims—Frank Sr. and Frank Jr.—out on the road with the Moto-Labs. They did great jobs. The sessions not only were of immense help to the garage and electrical men, but were excellent public relations and sales tools for us.

These and other favorable factors combined to paint a bright outlook. But again, fate was around the bend. Unexpected and prolonged trouble lay ahead!

Confrontation

San Francisco was a highly unionized city in the 1930s, noted for labor strife and strikes.

We had been fortunate. Our employees seemed satisfied. We endeavored to treat them as individual human beings, not just a band of workers. We went out of our way to be understanding and helpful when they came to us with problems. We paid salaries and wages commensurate with those in our industry.

We had not reckoned, however, with the power of union leaders and the force of the labor movement in San Francisco.

We hardly had become adjusted to our new building before both the AFL and CIO mounted an offensive to unionize our employees. This led to a strike on May 11, 1937 by those who had joined the CIO. It lasted until June 5 when, against orders from the union organizers, these employees gave up and joined the AFL. The period in between was one of upheaval and uncertainty, with our company caught in a disruptive web of fierce union rivalry.

Following that strike, the AFL demanded higher wages from us. We did not grant these immediately. Without warning, a second strike hit us on June 22. This, forced on *all* our employees by the AFL organizers, lasted until July 2. We knew that many of our employees were not in sympathy with the union or the strike. But they had no choice.

Nor did we. It was a case of giving in to demands or closing our doors. After all we had gone through to build the business, and with responsibilities to distributors, stockholders, and others, we knew we couldn't do the latter. Our only option was to try to make the best of a bad situation that had been thrust upon us.

With the payroll we now had to meet, the profit outlook was bleak. Competition for business in our industry ruled out raising prices to compensate for our heavier expenses. Moreover, the turbulence created by the labor situation forced us to discontinue selling shares of stock. Too, the financial squeeze we were in made it necessary to suspend payment of the 15-cents-a-share dividends we had been declaring quarterly since June of 1936.

But, as the old saying goes, hope springs eternal. We had to push ahead on the premise we could make things work out. With semi-annual sales trips east, NAPA regional conferences, and other activity, we continued to progress from a volume standpoint, though certainly not in net earnings.

Harsh Reality

In 1938, our labor rates were 50 percent higher than those of Delco, Auto-Lite, and other competitors in the Chicago area and in the East.

Operating at any kind of profit was out of the question. Although we resumed our 15-cents-a-share quarterly dividend in March of 1939, the financial picture was dark. Reluctantly, I had been reaching a decision that the only course open to us was to move out of San Francisco. On trips east, I had been looking into other cities that might be possible locations.

In May of 1939, the union made further demands. In meeting them, there was no way we could foresee of eking out profits essential to our survival. We had to move. There was absolutely no choice.

In retrospect, it was a bold decision under the circumstances that engulfed us at the time. The affairs of the company had become so entangled by the problems with the union that it was hard to keep hopelessness at bay.

The logical place to go was the Eastern Seaboard. This was a long way to transplant factory equipment and personnel. It meant giving up the warm ties all of us had in California. It involved adjusting to a completely different environment. It called for explanations to our stockholders, many of whom were small investors. They had remained with us during the dark days when we had to suspend dividend payments. Most were residents of California. It was almost as if we were deserting them, which of course we weren't, except in the geographical sense.

But move we must!

Selecting a Site

Several cities were considered. In analyzing all of them from a number of criteria, New Haven, Connecticut, consistently came out at the top.

It was an important manufacturing center. Producers of components needed for the manufacturing of our products were nearby. Major markets were in close proximity. Midway along the New York-Boston corridor, it had excellent rail and trucking facilities for shipments. The chamber of commerce went out of its way to be helpful in supplying information, in encouraging us to come, and in pledging support. Bank people were interested and receptive. And, not the least important, Connecticut was a lovely state, with fine educational, cultural, and homemaking advantages for families.

It should be noted that this last point had meaning for Beryl and me, as well as for the other families involved. Our two children, Jane and John, would be in elementary school.

Thus, in my own mind, there was no question that New Haven was the right city for our company and for the families and individuals who would be moving with it. But I felt there should be corroboration from another member of the firm. It was for this reason that Edwin S. Scheeline Jr., a director and treasurer, accompanied me on one of the trips east to look into sites. He concurred with the selection of New Haven.

Preparations

Once the decision about New Haven had been reached and agreed upon by the full board, we proceeded to enter into a lease for space that had been found on the fourth floor of a group of buildings at 220 East Street in the Connecticut city. This consisted of approximately 25,400 square feet. As the lease was being signed on September 25, 1939 to cover a 10-year period, it was difficult not to think of the new building we had designed and moved into with such great hope in San Francisco. But we knew New Haven was going to be good for us and to us.

In June, we had sold the Universal Molding Company to American Molding Company, and it was to remain in the San Francisco building. Since we then became a customer of American for our molded parts, at least an indirect tie to the building would be maintained.

It was necessary to raise capital to finance the move. Five prominent New Haven banks provided it through a loan not to exceed $50,000. The loan agreement was signed on September 16, 1939. I recall with much satisfaction that it was repaid by November of the following year.

Mrs. Mae Scheeline and her son Edwin decided not to leave San Francisco. They resigned their offices with the company and as directors. R.L. Bradford was elected a director and secretary, and Ben Lansdale, a director and treasurer. We were sorry that the Scheelines, so much a part of the company, would not be joining us in New Haven. But we understood their ties to California.

During October and November of 1939, the Cleveland branch was moved to New Haven. Ben Lansdale came on from San Francisco to supervise setting up the new factory. It was not until 1940, however, that the San Francisco plant and offices were moved.

Closing Out

Our new offices were established officially in New Haven at the beginning of 1940. Work hadn't been finished on the quarters we were to occupy and our furniture hadn't arrived from San Francisco, but we made do with makeshift equipment.

Several office employees and their families made the move.

It then was time to go about getting equipment transported across the country and closing the San Francisco operation.

In April, Hans Geschossmann, an expert machinist who had been with the company for many years, arrived in New Haven to set up the machinery in the new factory and get production under way. Hans elected to stay in California, though, and returned there as soon as this work was completed.

It was in April also that Beryl and I arrived with our family. My brother Victor and others had come in February.

In closing the San Francisco plant, we disposed of all our gear-cutting machinery. This meant the company's production now was concentrated entirely on ignition parts and testing equipment. And they were doing well in the marketplace.

Echlin was in a new home. Sometimes there was a feeling that we somehow were starting all over. Yet we weren't. A quarter of a century had gone by since I went out to collect some bills for Earl's auto repair shop. In those 25 years we had built a business that had won an important niche in our industry.

Our annual volume had reached $500,000 and we had 50 people on our payroll. These figures seem small by today's standards. But they were credible numbers for a growing business in 1940.

So, the only sense in which we really were starting afresh was that of leaving old problems behind to move forward in a new location with faith and confidence in our company and its future.

War clouds were gathering for our nation. Who could know precisely what was ahead? But one thing we did know. Echlin was here to stay!

The War Years

Chapter 5
The War Years

Settling In

Things went well our first year in New Haven.

There was a natural period of adjustment. And we weren't without incidents. In February of 1941, we even had a fire break out in the courtyard next to our building. It threatened our floor for a while, but the New Haven Fire Department got it under control without serious damage to us.

On the whole, though, we had adapted comfortably and were showing profits again. On March 15 of that year we were able to pay a dividend on our preferred stock, the first since our move.

Furthermore, we added to our products by taking over the dimmer and stoplight switch business of Balkamp, Inc., an Indianapolis concern.

Another positive was the sale of our building in San Francisco. This had been on the market for some time. Finally, it was sold in September of 1941. From the standpoint of physical ties, San Francisco now was entirely behind us.

So, we were happy with our move to New Haven. And we were becoming involved in Connecticut activities. For instance, in addition to membership in the New Haven Chamber of Commerce, we joined the New Haven County Manufacturers Association, and I enjoyed participating personally in educational work on behalf of private industry. Also, we became members of the Connecticut branch of the National Metal Trades Association. I was pleased to serve as its president a few years later.

But in 1941 there was no way we could be unaware that the future was shrouded with uncertainty. France had fallen the year before in Europe. England was undergoing merciless bombardment. Flames from sinking ships ignited the Atlantic sea lanes.

For the company, America's national defense program was making itself felt. Raw materials were becoming increasingly scarce. We had to search for suppliers. What was down the road . . . for us, for everybody?

December 7, 1941. Pearl Harbor. The answer came with the bombs that fell from the skies on that fateful day.

America was at war across two oceans. What until then had been a national defense program became a war program—an all-out war program!

Accent on Production

When President Roosevelt announced war production goals for 1942 and 1943, it was difficult to visualize their ever being met. Enormous, almost unbelievable, numbers of aircraft, ships, tanks, and all manner of other materiel were needed to equip the armed forces.

It was a tribute to American manufacturing genius that the goals were achieved. An immense network of subcontractors turning out components, and prime contractors molding components into finished war materials, performed what is recognized to this day as an incredible miracle of production.

Our company's normal production was classified by the government as an essential industry. There were two reasons for this. One, our products were needed in a wide range of military vehicles. Two, with production of new cars suspended, existing cars had to run longer. That meant more replacement parts to keep the home front on wheels in order to perform the production miracle.

We felt, though, that we should extend our facilities to include production of other war materials. We were able to do this by manufacturing component parts for automatic airplane pilots. The prime contractor was Jack & Heintz of Cleveland, a company that made quite a name for itself through its extensive war work. Ben Lansdale, who resigned as treasurer and a director in June of 1942 to accept an army commission, played an instrumental role in obtaining other war work for us. All told, operating three shifts, we had some 150 employees in war production.

During this time, except to maintain connections in the field, there was little need for salesmen. Resignations to enter the armed services or direct war work with other companies had cut our sales force to a minimum. Only seven were left. Those capable of giving technical information to the trade and to military services became, in effect, engineers, and were so designated.

Meanwhile, I was asked to be a member of the Advisory Committee to the War Production Board in Washington, D.C. One of the committee's responsibilities was to determine quantities of crucial metals, such as copper, steel, and tungsten, needed for production of war materials, and to assure their adequate supply.

The work involved numerous meetings in Washington. Much personal time and effort went into this voluntary service, but I was gratified to have the opportunity to be an active participant. The war production program was a massive effort, and our committee was at the heart of it.

Problems Again!

Involved and preoccupied as we were with the war effort, trouble erupted from within. What a shame to have had to bear and deal with it when there was so much of importance to do for the country!

It began with the filing of a lawsuit against the company on April 1, 1942. The plaintiff was a holder of some of our preferred stock, Josephine Mortensen of Alameda, California. She alleged mismanagement and failure to meet obligations to our stockholders.

It would take several pages to record the machinations, manipulations, deceits, and in-house turmoil that ensued over the next two years. The wonder is that the company was able to carry on through all the disruption it was forced to undergo.

What it all came down to was that Robert L. Bradford, who had arrived on the scene in 1935 with his motorstat invention, was pursuing a scheme he had hatched to take over the company.

As indicated earlier, we had given him part-time employment; he was destitute and could not wait for royalties to develop on the invention he had brought us. He displayed a great deal of ability in performing the part-time jobs he was assigned, was made a full-time member of the staff, and ultimately a director and officer.

What we did not know at the time, although we had checked him out, was that he had a criminal record and had served a sentence at San Quentin. When we did learn about this later, it was obvious that he had been clever about using as reference the employment record of another man by the same name.

In his scheme to take over Echlin, or destroy it if he couldn't succeed in that, he was equally clever. He was able to enlist stockholders, force us through them to elect confederates of his to the board, have more lawsuits lodged against us, and almost oust me.

We had thought our problems with the labor unions in San Francisco were turbulent. They didn't reach the intensity of the upheavals and conspiracies we had to endure until finally, in 1944, we were able to rid ourselves of Bradford's co-conspirators and, in 1945, of Bradford himself.

This was the unhappiest, most disturbing chapter in Echlin's history. We were lucky to have pulled through it. Only the support of our own loyal directors, employees, and stockholders made it possible to do so. Much gratitude is due them for the fact that the company came out of this sorry series of episodes still intact.

The War's End

Through all the in-house turmoil we were able to maintain our war production. In addition to the War Production Board Committee, I had served as a member of an Office of Price Administration Advisory Committee. Until the war with Japan ended in August of 1945, Echlin had been heavily involved and had made significant contributions.

Now it was time to regroup. There was a pent-up demand for commodities that had been in short supply. Automobile production would be resumed. Once again, we would be able to get materials we needed for civilian production, although there would be a struggle until suppliers could get back to normal.

There was much to be done, but we entered the postwar era with confidence that growth would continue for Echlin.

Charles Claire Echlin, father of Earl, Jack, and Victor, aboard the family's first automobile, a curved-dash Oldsmobile, around 1903. Here began the Echlins' association with motor vehicles.

(L to R) Jack, Victor, and Earl Echlin with their mother Madeline at the family piano.

Earl C. Echlin, upon enlisting in the service during World War I.

Wireless License Given To Youth of Fifteen

Oakland Schoolboy Youngest in State to Pass United States Examination.

Jack Echlin, a fifteen-year-old school boy of Oakland, has the distinction of being the youngest person in California to pass the examination held by the United States Government officials for wireless telegraphy operators. He recently passed with high honors with a large class which took the examination.

Echlin's skill in the handling of wireless apparatus and his familiarity with the business has been learned from work on his own small plant erected at his home, 460 Vernon avenue, where he has studied enthusiastically each day after completing his work at the Grant School. He will graduate from the Grant School on Friday, and expects to become a pupil at the Manual Training and Commercial High School. The passing of the examination entitles him to accept any position where a wireless operator is required in an official capacity, but his family are insisting that he continue his studies and complete his school course.

With the small wireless plant with which he has been experimenting at home, young Echlin yesterday picked up a message from Honolulu. This was accomplished with the aid of an apparatus which he has invented and is now perfecting. This mechanism, when attached to the ordinary wireless plant, accentuates the sound produced by the receiving apparatus to such an extent as to make long distance messages sound as loud as those sent from but a few miles away.

A 1912 newspaper article highlighting Jack Echlin's early hobby.

Jack Echlin on board ship as a young wireless operator.

Beryl and Jack Echlin at Niagara Falls on their cross-country
automobile trip in 1928.

A three-story building was built in San Francisco in 1936-1937
to accommodate Echlin's growing business.

Echlin & Echlin, Inc., the first company logo, was established in 1924.

The Bear Brand, adopted from the California flag, was one of the first trademarks under which Echlin parts were sold.

Older parts, such as these coils and contact set, are still found on customers' shelves. Echlin has the largest offering of early model parts in the industry.

Echlin and NAPA began their affiliation in 1928, when NAPA named Echlin its exclusive supplier of oil-pump and igniter gears.

Echlin catalogues have been models for the industry since the late 1920s.

Carlyle Fraser, who built a jobbing business in Atlanta into the Genuine Parts Company. In addition to being a major customer, he was a large stockholder, director, and treasured friend of Echlin.

An early 1930s piece from the *San Francisco Daily News*,
which ran a series of editorials on area businessmen.

Echlin moved from San Francisco to this modest New Haven, Connecticut, facility in 1939/1940.

New Times, Resumed Growth

Chapter 6
New Times, Resumed Growth

Surveying the Scene

The period immediately following World War II was one of catch up for the nation and for the company. Making the transition back to a peacetime economy called for assessment of where we stood, what we needed to do, and the directions we wanted to travel.

The logical policy for us was to concentrate on filling pent-up need for our products, and, once filled, to continue expanding the markets in this and other countries. At the same time, in the interest of broad growth, we would be on the lookout for suitable products to add to those we already had.

This, then, was the course we set for ourselves.

As we pursued it late in 1945 and into 1946, there were changes in the top ranks of the company. Victor Echlin, who had done such a remarkable job in sales and other capacities, decided to leave to devote himself to interests he had developed. He was succeeded on the board by J. Rodman McCoy, who was a director and executive of the NAPA Philadelphia warehouse distributor.

It was at this time that Carlyle Fraser also was elected to our board. As indicated earlier, his company, Genuine Parts, was our largest customer. Through our close personal friendship and business ties, he had purchased a large block of stock in Echlin. As a director over the next several years, his active interest and wise counsel brought much to our company.

Our ties to NAPA also remained strong. In the 1940s, I became a member of its Manufacturers Council, and subsequently had the honor of serving for two years as chairman of this group.

On Course

In the spring of 1947, with our existing products doing well, we purchased the condenser business of Nord Manufacturing Company in Westport, Connecticut. The company produced a high-quality condenser for which we felt there was a good market. Nord had not, however, been able to obtain adequate financing to manufacture the item in quantity. Ernst A. Norberg, its president, came with us when we took over the operation.

Crowded office conditions were an indication of our growth. In October of 1947, a need for increased speed and efficiency led us to install IBM equipment. We did this in the room formerly occupied by our catalogue department. The catalogue department had to be moved to the general office, congesting that area to a point at which personnel literally were stepping over one another!

With business increasing and expanding, it was clear we needed more space. Fortunately, it became available on the third and fourth floors of the building we occupied on East Street. In the early part of 1948, we signed a lease for 48,000 square feet there, bringing our total in the building to a little more than 73,000 square feet.

Another sign of growth was our need for an advertising agency. We knew we had superior products. They were being marketed successfully. But we were conscious of the importance of adroit merchandising in maintaining present success, and expanding it to added success.

Friends at New Britain Machine recommended Humbert and Jones, a New York agency. We interviewed a number of different agencies, but followed our friends' recommendation. We soon were delighted that we had. Right from the beginning, King Humbert and Ralph Jones displayed unique talent in creating attention-attracting advertising for our company.

The Sparky ads were an early example. No artist ever drew a more provocative girl than the one to whom we gave the name Sparky after she began appearing in two-color Echlin product promotions in the industry's leading publications.

Sparky stepping out of a shower to illustrate that "Some parts must be protected against moisture!" No one could miss Sparky, the interior of an Echlin condenser there beside her, and the line "Just look at this construction" to emphasize that Echlin condensers were waterproof.

Sparky, with minimum covering, running toward the reader of the ad saying, "Oh, mister—here are some pointers on POINTS and profits!" Points indeed! Sparky's focused eyes on hers—and on copy about Echlin's ignition contacts: ". . . to make an extra profit on every job—watch those points— replace them with ECHLIN every time!"

It didn't take long for these and other ads in the series to become the talk of the trade . . . and to sell Echlin products. Humbert and Jones followed these with continuing excellent advertising, and grew so close to us that we considered them almost part of our organization.

Still another barometer of our expansion was a precedent we established in May of that year. We had a meeting of our salesmen from across the country. My office was our conference room. It was an especially good meeting. One of the reasons was that the men had been invited to bring their wives to New Haven. The idea proved a popular one. It was repeated at future meetings.

Progression and Progress

It is axiomatic that as sales continue to grow, close attention must be focused on maintaining quality while increasing quantity of production. We had an excellent man heading our production, Earl J. Sambrook, who had become plant manager in 1945. In April of 1949, emphasizing the importance we attached to his position and the operations he directed, Earl was made vice president in charge of production. He was the first vice president ever elected in our company.

With our financial picture steadily brightening, we also adopted a new dividend policy in 1949. Under this we began paying two back dividends, along with the one for the current quarter. This was something particularly satisfying to me. During past turbulent times we had had to suspend and forego dividend payments. Doing so had always worried and troubled me, and I was pleased that we now could begin making up for past omissions.

In the summer of that year, continuing to broaden our sphere, we bought the coil-winding department of Anaconda Wire & Cable Company in Muskegon, Michigan. The equipment arrived in October. Ralph Kern, who had been in charge of the department at Anaconda, was employed to come to New Haven to set up the machinery, train operators, and take permanent charge.

The year 1949 is especially memorable to me for an additional reason. At the NAPA annual meeting held in Hot Springs, Virginia, that September, we introduced what we called the Visumatic Sales and Service Program.

In 1944, I had an idea for a shelf divider for use by garages and repair shops. The framework was a cabinet. In it were series of compartments for organizing, containing, and displaying different sizes of ignition parts. Tabs at the back of the shelves showed parts numbers and recommended quantities to be stocked. These were to serve as an inventory control system. Designed, of course, to hold Echlin ignition parts, the device was conceived as a merchandising tool for the company.

At the time, with material scarcities because of the war, it was not possible to put the concept into production. But I patented it and earmarked it for the future.

That came in 1949. King Humbert gave it the name,

Visumatic. For the NAPA Hot Springs meeting, we had prepared a visual presentation, as well as catalogues and promotional literature.

We couldn't have asked for a more enthusiastic reception and response. Among the many favorable reactions voiced at the meeting was this statement by D.N. Test, a senior executive of the Boozer-Test Management Company, owners of 11 NAPA warehouses in the Midwest:

"This is, without doubt, the best merchandising program ever offered to NAPA. It is so good that it must be continued for three or four years at least to give it a chance for real success."

As things turned out, it didn't need the generous period of three to four years Mr. Test had advocated. The successs Visumatic quickly achieved and maintained brought it wide acclaim as what many users called "the outstanding merchandising plan of the replacement parts business."

The Disappearing Past

On the financial side, which always had been such a burdensome one, 1950 opened on a happy note.

In January, we paid all back dividends on our preferred stock. Simultaneously, we prepared to call all the preferred stock, which was done as of February 28. Since that date happened to coincide with my birthday, I remember it well!

In making the call, we gave stockholders a choice. One was to accept $11.00 a share plus a 15-cent dividend for the quarterly period ending February 28. Or, they could convert their shares of preferred stock to common on a basis of share for share.

Considerable capital was needed for all this, and we decided to negotiate a loan of $200,000 to help underwrite it.

My strategy in obtaining this amount of money was to approach three possible sources: The Prudential Insurance Company, Newark, New Jersey; the Irving Trust Company in New York; and The New Haven Bank, NBA. The hope was that at least one of the three would be willing to grant the loan.

What a pleasant surprise! All three said yes!

Our decision was to accept Irving Trust's offer, in that we had been banking with them for some time. The terms called for repaying it over a five-year period.

What a delightful experience it was to repay that loan *in full out of earnings* three months later!

When the preferred stock call was made on February 28, 13,272 of the shares were converted by their owners to shares of common. We were pleased with the confidence these shareholders showed in the future of the company, and are equally pleased today that they have been rewarded over the years with substantial appreciation in the value of their holdings.

There are two interesting footnotes to this call of preferred stock.

One was a letter received some months later from Mr. D.S. Bush, supervisory appraiser, Prudential Insurance Company. It opened with these words:

"This note may serve to remind of Prudential's standby interest in any financing prospects that may develop . . ."

For someone who, with hat in hand, had gone to lenders so many times in the past to plead for loans, this was the sweetest of music! Whether we ever might wish to take advantage of it was incidental. A major insurance company actually was standing by with interest in financing us!

The other footnote concerns a trip to California Mrs. Pardo made in the summer of that year.

As stated earlier, our reason for issuing stock in 1936 was to raise money for the new building we needed. During her visit in San Francisco that summer of 1950, Mrs. Pardo, for old times' sake, decided to drive past the building. As she arrived at the corner of 16th and Vermont, she was astounded! The building had disappeared!

Mrs. Pardo found out that the building had been razed for a new viaduct. But what an amazing coincidence it was! The structure preferred stock had helped finance was gone. Now, so was the preferred stock.

A Look Into the Future

Progress continued in 1951, although the nation was at war again, this time in Korea. That conflict in no way approached the magnitude of World War II, however, and shortages of critical materials were not a significant factor.

Once again, I was called on to attend meetings in Washington, D.C., and to devote time to other matters related to the war. This came about through having been asked to become a member of the Automotive Replacement Parts Manufacturers Industry Advisory Committee of the Office of Price Stabilization and the National Production Authority. As before, I was pleased to do my part in aiding the war effort.

In September of that year, we took what perhaps was viewed as a bold action by running a 28-page insert in *Jobber Topics*, the jobbers' trade publication. This paid off in the attention it attracted, and the favorable nationwide comment it drew as an innovative way of advertising our company and its products.

This followed a letter I had written in August to all of our salesmen. There was a definite connection between the two, as is seen in these quotes from the letter:

"The early part of 1951 set all-time high records for sales. From certain facts we have, we believe we took another step ahead of the ignition parts industry. Echlin Manufacturing Company has for many years been increasing its volume faster than the general market for ignition parts.

"In addition to past history, I would like to mention that we are not operating this business on a basis of fear of war with Russia, nor with fear of shortages of material or labor. We are continuing our plant expansion and our aggressive sales methods. These include some expansion of our sales force and some special effort where needed, as well as some

very impressive and actually startling advertising you will
see in the near future."

Emphasis on Sales

Ever since the Frank Beckman days of 1927, selling has
been of strong interest to me. As the letter stated, we were
running ahead of our competition in the industry. We had
every intention of staying ahead, and an effective sales force
held the key.

Any sales organization needs new injections of vitality
from time to time to maintain it at a top level of productivity.
In 1952, we moved Elmer Lillie, who had been with us for
more than 20 years and had done outstanding work in the
Pacific Northwest, to New Haven. He took over as sales
promotion manager.

At the same time, we inaugurated a system of counselors.
Senior men especially qualified to advise and help
individuals in charge of sales territories were assigned to
such work. This proved to be a good move. The counselors
were able to assist in overcoming obstacles or problems that
arose. Further, their support and expertise gave our salesmen added confidence and capability.

In September of that year, to supplement the bolstering of
our sales organization, we took another bold advertising step.
This was a 16-page presentation of our product line in *Motor
Magazine*, the leading automotive industry publication.

A letter from the president of the Hearst Corporation,
publishers of the magazine, made us proud of that
advertisement and of our advertising agency, Humbert and
Jones, which had prepared it. The letter said:

> "I write you this note to offer my congratulations
> for one of the soundest and most dramatic pieces
> of advertising that it has been the privilege of any
> of the Hearst Publications to carry in a long time.
> It is an idea like yours that sells goods and builds
> a business."

Again, there was excellent response. Echlin products were in the limelight. And they were selling.

Production: Keeping Pace

As sales were expanded, we simultaneously concentrated on efficient factory operations.

New machinery adapted to the specialized needs of the company's manufacturing processes had been built on the premises. Much of this was done by an expert machine designer we had employed, Louis Ryman, who had worked with Igor Sikorsky in the development of the helicopter. His machines, along with others designed by Ernst Norberg, increased our efficiency and output.

Virtually all phases of manufacturing contacts were handled at the plant, with careful inspection from start to finish.

Condensers were wound on automatic machines Ernie had designed. Almost the entire operation of producing water-proof condensers, now manufactured exclusively by the company, took place on the fourth floor.

Windings for our coils were produced and assembled on the second floor. On this same floor, presses turned out about 90 percent of our molded parts and molded items for other manufacturers.

Our power press department was on the third floor. Max Kvit was in charge of this. Max had been with us since a short time after we had taken over the J.J. Schnerr operation in San Francisco. As a young man, he had just immigrated to the United States from Russia and applied to us for his first job in this country. We gave him one in the shop. He was a loyal and skilled worker who moved with us to New Haven and spent his entire career with Echlin until he retired a few years ago.

Our shipping operations were also on the third floor.

Too, we had what we called a changeover department. Merchandise from jobbers who had converted to the Echlin line was reboxed and renumbered there.

Equipment, of course, is efficient only to the degree that it has skilled individuals operating it. We were so fortunate in this regard. Many of our factory employees had been with us since we moved to New Haven in 1940. They were skilled in our operations and superb instructors of new employees.

How Far Had We Come?

There was every reason to be pleased with our progress since World War II. We had a line of quality products, a top-grade sales organization, an efficient factory, and steadily rising volume.

When my wonderful secretary of 25 years, Mrs. Pardo, retired in 1953, we talked about the quarter of a century we had worked together—the ups and downs, the trials and tribulations. But, most of all, we talked about the good things—the positives had so far outweighed the negatives that we now could smile about many of the latter.

The good things indeed. We had so much for which to be grateful. Echlin had traveled a long way. Just a relatively short time before Mrs. Pardo joined us in 1928, we had struggled to reach a break-even point of $120,000 a year in volume. In 1953, as we said good-by, our annual volume was close to $3,500,000.

Patterns Of Expansion

Chapter 7
Patterns Of Expansion

Multi-Faceted Growth

The next few years witnessed continuous expansion in all directions for Echlin.

Our volume of sales in the United States kept climbing. We moved ahead on broader fronts in the international markets. We added products. We consistently needed more space and provided it to take care of our rising production. We opened facilities in other parts of the country. Our number of employees rose.

We were becoming a big company!

Always we had maintained confidence that we would grow, that our future was bright, even when we were passing through some of the dark periods. But we probably hadn't envisioned the magnitude to which this would be true.

It was an exciting time, a time of satisfaction with what had been accomplished, yet one of enthusiastically looking ahead to achieving new goals, reaching greater heights.

How often I wished that Earl could have been there to see where his little auto repair shop had led us, and where we still were going!

Our Neighbor to the North

For some time during the 1930s and 1940s, we had been doing a fair amount of business in Canada, and had built good customers there. By 1950, however, difficulties had arisen. The Canadian government had imposed restrictions on importations, including our products.

That year I had gone to Ottawa to see what, if anything, might be done to change the situation. An extremely helpful attorney we had retained, Harold Mayne Daly, K.C., arranged for me to meet with a number of government officials. But nothing really developed from these sessions. The government was adamant in its stand on imports.

Although we continued to do some business in Canada under this handicap, we knew we were having to forego important volume that could be obtained there.

Finally, in 1954, we overcame the problem by organizing our own Canadian company, Echlin Ignition of Canada, Ltd.

This proved to be a productive move. It enabled us to begin reaching into the potential markets we knew existed in that great country.

We followed this by organizing a Western Hemisphere corporation, the Echlin Sales Company. We were aware that there was business to be built both to the north and south of the United States. This was one of the vehicles for doing so.

Again, a Need for Space

With volume continuing upward, we again were out-growing our space in the New Haven building.

A recurring thought was that perhaps we should have a factory building of our own. We had followed this route in San Francisco. Had unforeseen labor problems not forced us to move away, it would have been ideal for our purposes. Perhaps it was time to try again.

We made a positive decision accordingly. After looking at and studying a number of possible sites, we selected a piece of property that was on the market in nearby Branford. We bought it in 1956 and designed a building with 70,700 square feet of floor space.

The new quarters were completed in 1957, and we moved in that year.

A measure of our progressive growth can be seen in the

fact that this space was adequate for only a short time. We had to build an addition which was completed in 1959, giving us a total of 107,000 square feet.

It was at the time this expansion was occurring that Doug Williams joined the company. He came to us in 1956 and quickly demonstrated the unusual ability one seeks in a member of the top management team. Doug, made vice president in 1957, was a vital part of our organization as we progressed over the next several years.

Staying in Touch

There can be a family atmosphere in a small business— a warmth between management and employees that makes the company's success a common objective. That certainly was the case at the building on East Street in New Haven, where all of us worked so close to one another.

One who likes people takes a personal interest in them, and I continuously had done this with our employees. They knew they always could talk with me, whether about their work, or about situations and problems in their families or other aspects of their personal lives. The larger a company grows, the more difficult this naturally becomes, but at our expanded office and factory in Branford, I endeavored to maintain the same policy. The door of my corner office always was open. If during the course of a busy day there was no opportunity to talk with an employee who had come to me with a problem, the two of us would stay after closing hours to discuss it and find a way of working it out.

Another long-practiced policy was to get out on the factory floor to observe firsthand how everything was going. It wasn't a matter of checking up on people. Rather, I wanted to stay in close touch with production. There can be a tendency to lose contact with this vital phase of the business when so many other things needing attention come across one's desk every day.

From those factory-floor visits, I developed a reputation

longtime employees remind me about—and we have a chuckle over it—to this day.

It was what they say was an uncanny knack for picking up and examining, from an entire batch of just-produced parts, the single one that for some reason or another had an imperfection, however slight.

I remember one time finding such an item that was about to be boxed. It got me so concerned that I had the employees unbox every one in a large stack. It was some scene—all those items being scrutinized, all those empty boxes! But I wanted to be certain. Only recently I was talking with Burt Sibley who had been part of that scene. We joked about the pandemonium and how relieved we all were when we could find nothing else that was wrong.

Periodic loudspeaker messages were another means of communicating with the employees. We had installed a speaker system throughout the plant, and there was a microphone in my office.

At first, I used it for announcements of various kinds—important news events, developments of significance to our company, holiday information, and the like. These evolved into little talks, usually three to five minutes, about company matters. The idea was to keep everybody informed about how we were doing, what we were planning, and where we were heading.

These brief talks became a part of our working together as a company. Whenever I visit the Branford plant, employees who were there those years ago mention them to me.

Widened Ownership

Meanwhile, other historical things were happening.

For example, it also was in 1959 that Echlin became a Connecticut corporation. All those years since 1940 we had maintained our California corporation. With Connecticut to remain our home, it made sense to have our corporate base there as well. The California corporation was dissolved.

With our rapid growth, safeguarding the company's perpetuity should anything happen to Carlyle Fraser or me, the two largest stockholders, became increasingly important. As a means of accomplishing this, Carlyle and I made a decision to sell substantial portions of our stock to the public. This enabled us to establish a fund for inheritance tax purposes.

The sale was handled by Blair & Company, a prominent Wall Street investment banking firm. The stock was first offered in April of 1959 at $16.50 per share. Immediately, it began to rise. Many NAPA warehouse people, NAPA jobbers, others in the industry, and individuals in financial circles aware of the company and its products were anxious to acquire shares.

How gratifying it was to observe how well they were rewarded for their confidence. It wasn't long until the original offering price had doubled. Within two years, the value had more than tripled. And in August of 1961, Echlin stock was split 2 for 1 in the form of a 100 percent stock dividend.

A Desire, An Opportunity

Beryl and I long had taken a special interest in education and health, contributing to them within our ability to do so. Proceeds from the sale of Echlin stock made it possible for us to pursue this interest in a much broader way.

The proceeds were used to establish the Echlin Foundation. A trust agreement under which Beryl, John, and I serve as trustees was signed in December of 1959.

Every year since then, the foundation has made grants to or underwritten projects for selected educational institutions, libraries, hospitals, and other agencies. A few examples will suffice to illustrate specific grantees. They include:

- Saint Raphael's Hospital in New Haven.
- Mercy Hospital in Independence, Kansas, used by many Echlin employees in that area.
- Boca Raton Community Hospital in Florida. A pharmacy and other facilities have been made possible by the foundation.

- The Carlyle Fraser Heart Center in Atlanta. Affiliated with the Emory University Crawford Long Hospital, this excellent facility stands as a memorial to our great friend and colleague, and we have been pleased to have the opportunity of contributing to it.
- The Blackstone Memorial Library in Branford, Connecticut, as well as the Branford Hospice, one of the first in the nation.
- Quinnipiac Council, Boy Scouts of America, Hamden, Connecticut.
- The Florence Fuller Center for Underprivileged Children, Boca Raton.
- The University of New Haven.

No pleasure could exceed what we have derived from being able to share Echlin's good fortune as a company, and ours personally, with these and many other foundation recipients.

A Major Merger

Down through the years, a close and favorable association had developed between Echlin and the United Parts Manufacturing Company of Chicago. United manufactured brake parts and was the supplier of these to NAPA.

Along the line, Echlin had offered its Visumatic program to other factories distributing their parts through NAPA, and United had been among those that quickly took advantage of the opportunity to benefit from adopting the program. This, together with other common interests and objectives, clearly suggested that significant benefits could accrue from closer commercial ties between the two companies.

The more the potentials were considered, the more we realized that a merger would be desirable for both. Consequently, we entered into negotiations, arriving at final terms approved by the stockholders of the two companies late in 1959. The actual merger took place on January 4, 1960.

The brake part manufacturing operations were continued in Chicago. The sales forces of the two organizations were combined into one, and Echlin now had a United Parts Division.

An indication of the impact the merger had on Echlin's volume can be seen in the fact that our net sales for fiscal year 1960, ending August 31, were $14,328,217, almost $6,000,000 more than in the previous year.

Other Developments

In 1960, we expanded our Canadian operations to include products of the new United Parts Division. At the same time, we changed the name of our Canadian company to Echlin-United of Canada, Ltd.

An important occurrence in 1961 was the adding of Raybestos and Grey-Rock to our list of customers. Another was the purchase of property in Elk Grove, Illinois, near O'Hare Airport, to build a new plant which we occupied the following year.

With 1961 came sadness, too. Our close friend and associate, Carlyle Fraser, passed away. As a major customer, as a director and officer of our company, as a large stockholder, Carlyle's contributions to Echlin were manifold.

Genuine Parts was fortunate in having a man of Wilton Looney's caliber move up to the company's chairmanship, succeeding Carlyle. So were we. Wilton has done a marvelous job for Genuine Parts and for the entire industry. He is deserving in every way of the high regard in which he is so widely held. He is a good friend of our company, a warm, personal friend.

In 1962, carburetor parts were added to our line. And again, we were bursting at the seams as far as space was concerned.

We met the need for space by adding a building to our Branford plant. This brought our total there to 138,000 square feet. The number of persons employed at the plant grew to approximately 620.

A Milestone Year

On January 1, 1963, Fred Mancheski joined our company as vice president, manufacturing and engineering. As an executive of one of the large management consulting firms, Fred had worked with us on a number of matters. It was plain he had ideas and talents which could be of value to us on a continuing basis.

We were happy to have him become a part of our organization. As events of the future unfolded, the day he came with us was one of destiny for Fred and for Echlin.

It was noted previously that we were becoming a big company. This was increasingly true. And opportunities were developing for us to grow far beyond the point we had reached. They were opportunities, however, that would require much more capital than our profits could underwrite or that we could expect to borrow from banks or other lenders.

In fact, there was only one way to raise the amount of money we really would need to move in the directions open to us. That was to go public in a major way.

The New York Stock Exchange. Yes, that was our answer. Echlin shares on the Big Board.

In 1959, when Carlyle Fraser and I put our blocks of stock up for sale to the public, the shares were traded in the over-the-counter market. Echlin remained in that market until 1962, then went onto the American Stock Exchange.

Our stock's performance over the counter and on the American Stock Exchange had been good. Our affairs were in excellent shape. Our business outlook was extremely bright. So, we had no difficulty in getting a primary underwriter to make the preparations for our move to the Big Board.

Days spent in New York working with our brokers to get ready for a momentous event in our history were enlightening and exhilarating. There is an aura about Wall Street. One is exposed directly to dealings in sums of money commonplace there, but staggering in comprehension outside. To say the least, it was an interesting experience—at times, it was even a bit hard to believe it was happening.

Here was Echlin, about to join company with the nation's greatest corporations in being listed on the New York Stock Exchange. There was an unmistakable touch of magic about it.

What a moment it was! Our son John and I were there when Echlin's stock symbol, ECH, first flashed on that board! I bought the first 100 shares; John the second 100. The date was March 4, 1963. People in all walks of life, large and small investors alike, were about to join us as partners in reaching out to the opportunities that stretched before us.

It was a day of celebration and of bright promise. Yet, it also was a day of reflection and gratitude.

Advancing on Broad Fronts

In June of 1963, a little more than five months after coming with the company, Fred Mancheski became a director. In October of that year, he was given added responsibilities as vice president and general manager.

Thus was molded between us a close and harmonious relationship that remains to this day.

In 1964, with the capital to move faster and more widely than had been possible until then, we proceeded with a number of actions.

One was to purchase the voltage regulator business of Electra Manufacturing Company of Independence, Kansas. The Automotive Controls Corporation was organized to operate this enterprise.

Another acquisition was Chimont Machined Products Company in Montague, Michigan. This was followed by the purchase of the Arrow-Newaygo Foundry Company in Newaygo, Michigan. Then came Otto Items in St. Louis, Missouri.

As can be seen, we were gaining quite a manufacturing

presence in the Midwest.

Our Canadian business was expanding, too. We found it advantageous to build a plant there. This was a special project undertaken by our son John, then with the company, and he did outstanding work in planning and executing it.

From making an initial, in-depth cost study, to selecting Rexdale, Ontario, as the location, personally negotiating with government officials, and supervising construction and installing of machinery, he did a thorough and effective job.

The plant was completed and occupied in 1964. We soon were manufacturing about 50 percent of our Canadian ignition requirements and 20 percent of our brake parts in the new factory. And the following year we enlarged it to handle even more of our production.

It also was in 1964 that I resigned as president of the company and was elected chairman. Fred Mancheski, continuing his well-earned moves upward, was elected president.

An Outside Asset

At this juncture, the University of New Haven is deserving of a place in the Echlin story.

A close association with this fine institution, now a fully accredited four-year university, then a struggling two-year college specializing in engineering and business, began in 1962.

I remember a visit from Larry Parker that year. The college had established a School of Executive Development, which he headed. This offered a two-year certificate for middle managers from companies in the New Haven area. Larry hoped to recruit some of our people for the course.

What he had to say interested me. Here, I learned, was a school making it possible for young people unable to afford heavy tuition fees to obtain basic education in engineering and business. It merited help.

We responded by enrolling some of our middle managers in the course and found they benefited greatly from it. Dr. Marvin K. Peterson, who then was president, and I became good friends, and I began taking an active overall interest in the school. This led to my being elected to the board of governors and serving on it until 1972.

During this time, as a member of the finance committee, there were opportunities for me to advise and assist in obtaining increased funding for the college. Dr. Phillip Kaplan, who succeeded Marvin as president in 1973, and I also became good friends as my interest continued.

This interest extended to the Echlin Foundation's playing a major financial role in the 1981 purchase of a former AT&T building near the campus. This became a computer center for academic and administrative functions at the university. The building now is known as Echlin Hall.

And something I treasure a great deal is an Honorary Doctor of Business Administration degree awarded to me by the university in 1981.

Beryl and I maintain a scholarship fund for undergraduate students in engineering and business, and John continues active family participation as a member of the board of governors.

Employee Participation

There is an old maxim that a company is as good as its management. That's true only up to a point. Good as management may be, its performance hinges to a crucial degree on the skill and workmanship of those who produce the products out on the factory floors.

Even back in the trying days of the labor union battles in San Francisco, Echlin had loyal employees. This was true through the trials and tribulations of the Bradford era. All along, we had benefited from the interest, dedication, and skills of our factory people.

It was only fitting, then, that they be given an opportunity to participate with our office, sales, and other employees in sharing the dividends of our combined efforts. So, in 1965 we instituted a stock purchase plan for all employees.

It was gratifying to see the number who responded to this offer. And it is all the more gratifying to know that, over the years, their investments have been sound and profitable.

The Widening Network

Our base was broadened still further in 1965. We purchased a transmission parts business, and acquired a switch line from Balkamp.

Also, with our ignition line expanding, David C. Miller came with the company that year as ignition sales manager. Dave had an excellent knowledge of electrical products and later, as a corporate vice president, was general manager of our electrical products group.

In 1966, we bought property in McHenry, Illinois, to build a plant there for handling more of our Midwest production.

That same year, we added small engine parts to our line. Meanwhile, we moved our Solenoid Division, which had been located in Chicago, to our Independence, Kansas, plant. Some 280 persons now were employed in our Voltage Regulator and Solenoid Division.

There was a lot of activity. We had put our new capital to work. And it was working productively for us.

In November of 1966, we again expanded our product offering. We added new carburetors, which were built and supplied to us by original equipment manufacturers.

Early in 1967, we arranged to purchase Peerless Motor Products Company, manufacturers of wire assemblies, to add to our Canadian operations. This was completed the next year.

In April of 1967, our Chimont Machined Products Company was moved from Montague, Michigan, to our new plant at McHenry where employment reached 225. Later, Chimont was consolidated with Brake Parts Company.

Too, we were expanding in foreign countries. Ernie Lenz had done outstanding work as our export manager in New York. Now it was time to establish our own self-contained international organization. We did this in 1967.

William J. O'Grady joined the company to head the international operations. Bill was just the right man for this work and did a superb job of getting our products into an increasing number of countries. Later, he became marketing director of Echlin International. With many pleasant visits in our home after I retired, we remained warm, personal friends.

Through Bill's work, we soon had sales representatives in 26 different countries. These included South America (except Brazil), Australia, Indonesia, Korea, New Zealand, Philippines, South Africa, Thailand, and Viet Nam.

Moreover, we were entering new fields with product lines.

For example, after a market and manufacturing study of small engine and other parts for lawn mowers, we began the manufacture of these in April of 1967. In 1968, we launched production on valves, carburetor parts, ignition parts, spark plugs, piston rings and additional parts for outboard engines. The manufacturing and marketing of these were placed with a new subsidiary, Sierra Supply Company, based in Litchfield, Illinois.

With this continued expansion, we also did some organizational restructuring to simplify and improve our operations.

Two steps were taken. The first was to concentrate production of electrical and fuel system parts in a single subsidiary company, Automotive Controls Corporation (ACC). The second was to consolidate our manufacturing of brake parts in another subsidiary, Brake Parts Company.

Eyes on Europe

In 1967, we also were looking ahead to having plants in other countries. This was illustrated by a trip Beryl and I made to England that year.

A company of our type, Park Brothers, was located in Blackburn. Fred and Kenneth Park had built it into a leading manufacturer of replacement parts for the electrical and ignition systems of British-made automobiles. In addition, the firm did a substantial export business in Europe.

Echlin had a pleasant relationship with Park Brothers. We hoped that some day it might become directly affiliated with us. This it did in 1973 with our acquisition of the company, though I'm sorry to add that unforeseeable difficulty lay ahead for it after that.

The purpose of our trip was to become more closely acquainted with Fred and Kenneth Park, their operation, and their plans for the future.

What a delightful visit it was!

Kenneth Park met us in Manchester with his Silver Shadow Rolls Royce. We drove to their home in Whalley, near Blackburn, for lunch with him and his family, and later to meet the Fred Park family.

The house, directly facing on the sidewalk in front of it, was 250 years old, with stone walls 21½ inches thick. We never had seen anything quite like this and were fascinated by it.

There were productive talks with the Park brothers. And they and their families entertained us in so many gracious ways. We became warm, lasting friends.

The visit was not without some interesting sightseeing. The ruins of Bolton Abbey near Harrowgate were one of the highlights. Beryl was given a 400-year-old piece of Roman brick from the ruins, as well as an 800-year-old piece of glazed glass. They became long-kept mementos.

And Beryl was especially pleased to see the Devonshire area where her father was born. She even got to visit with the widow of an uncle, and with a cousin and his wife. The Goldsworthy family went back a long way in that part of England.

A Successful Transition

Chapter 8
A Successful Transition

A Time Had Come

More than half a century had passed since that December day in 1915 when I stopped by my brother Earl's auto repair shop and went out to collect some bills for him.

Years back, there had been a famous advertisement for Fisk tires. It showed a little boy beside a tire. Dressed in night clothes and holding a candle, he was ready for bed. The tagline was "It's Time To Retire."

That line applied to me those years later. While I wanted to maintain some degree of participation in the affairs of the company, it was time to step down as chairman.

Echlin's house was in good order.

We were moving ahead on all fronts. We had an ever-growing group of fine products. Our production facilities were modern and efficient. We had wonderful employees at all levels of management and in our plants. Our distributor organization was unsurpassed in the industry. We were making money. We had no indebtedness.

And as to leaving the company in good hands, Fred Mancheski certainly had demonstrated expert capability in every aspect of heading the corporation.

In my mind, then, I set 1969 as the year for making the transition. And a telephone call one night toward the end of 1968 opened a perfect opportunity for getting it under way.

The call was from some good friends, Karl and Eleanor Finsterbusch. They wanted Beryl and me to join them on a round-the-world cruise that was to leave New York the middle of January and was to take three-and-a-half months.

Our friendship with them (Karl was an engineer with Stone and Webster in New York) had begun aboard ship on an earlier cruise. At any time in the past, the thought of being away for three-and-a-half months would have been inconceivable to me. But not now. What better way to start the transition than by letting Fred have a run on his own at the helm?

Coincidentally, the cruise route showed Cape Town, South Africa, as one of the ports of call. At the company, we had been exploring the possibility of acquiring a manufacturing facility in South Africa. Some business could be mixed with pleasure when we got there.

A New Experience

The ship was the S.S. Rotterdam, of the Holland-American Line. Over the three-and-a-half-month period, it was to take us almost 32,000 miles.

From New York, we would go down through the Caribbean to South America, stopping at Rio de Janeiro. Then, it was across the Atlantic to South Africa. From there, we would travel up the east coast of Africa. Stops in India would be next, followed by southeast Asia, including Singapore, Bangkok, and Hong Kong. Kobe and Yokohama in Japan were on the schedule before crossing the Pacific to Honolulu. San Francisco was our destination from Hawaii, then down to Acapulco, on to the Panama Canal, and back to New York.

Beryl and I had been on other cruises, but none in any way approaching the length of this one. Aboard and underway on the Rotterdam, my emotions were a bit mixed. I was looking forward to every part of the trip. But being away from the office for that long! Could a pattern of 53 years be changed this quickly? Would I be able to keep from making transoceanic telephone calls?

We were embarking on an exciting journey to see the

world, and the office had to be left behind. With Fred in full charge, Echlin could get along without my keeping in touch. After all, I was supposed to be retiring.

The office did get along.

There was only one transoceanic call along the way. That was from Fred. A decision had to be made on a major matter and he wanted to know what I thought about it. After we talked briefly, I had but one comment:

"You're in charge, Fred. Only one person should make this decision. That's you. I know it will be a good one."

It was a good one, too. There was no doubt about Fred's ability. And I wasn't doing badly either!

A Pleasant Assignment

After arriving in Cape Town, the Finsterbusches and Beryl and I left the ship for a week. We arranged to rejoin it at Lorenco Marques, up the east coast of Africa. From Cape Town, we flew to Johannesburg.

The company in which we were interested was called Charger. It rebuilt starters, alternators, and generators. The firm was headed by Hyman Marcus. He and his brother were the owners.

As mentioned earlier, Echlin had been looking into the possibility of acquiring the company. We had retained a consultant to analyze the potentials South Africa offered us, and his report had been highly favorable. Charger would give us the base we needed for developing a manufacturing facility there. It would be our first international production site outside of Canada.

Hymie Marcus and his family couldn't have entertained us more cordially or royally. We were given the feeling of being genuinely welcome in South Africa.

Two days of business discussions led to a preliminary agreement, subject to further negotiation, for Echlin to obtain a 50 percent interest in Charger. Beryl and I returned later in the year to consummate the deal. Within two years, our company became the majority owner, and the name was changed to Echlin Charger. Cecil Stewart, who had been sales manager and who impressed us as being an extremely capable man, was named general manager.

Over the years since, Echlin Charger has been built into one of our top international operations. It employs some 500 South Africans, and contributes an important share of our total company volume.

So Much To See

The rest of the week was spent sightseeing. The highlight was a three-day safari in Krueger Park, South Africa's large game reserve. What a marvelous experience it was! We enjoyed it so much that Beryl and I went on three more safaris during later trips to that country.

Becoming completely absorbed in wonderful things we were seeing on the cruise told me something encouraging about myself. While Echlin never was very far from my mind, I could switch it off to enjoy other things. That presented a good outlook for retirement.

This was clear from an occurrence in India after we had witnessed the splendor of the Taj Mahal at Agra. A short distance away, a camel was meandering along behind his drover. Karl Finsterbusch and I couldn't resist each taking a turn on that camel's back.

When I was astride the desert animal having my picture taken, I couldn't help saying to myself, "Can this be Jack Echlin?"

Never mind the somersault I took when he suddenly got down—front legs first—to let me off!

The cruise continued to be enjoyable in every respect. Singapore, Bangkok, Hong Kong, the ports in Japan we visited—all were as absorbing and fascinating as we had imagined they would be.

To view rituals and traditions that had been preserved over so many centuries was to be impressed with the strength and continuity of Oriental cultures. To observe how modern business methods and practices were so efficiently coexisting with those cultures was to foresee continuously rising prominence for East Asia in international commerce.

As a sidelight, one episode became a special conversation piece for me, despite skepticism from the other three members of our party.

In Hong Kong, a must for visitors was to stand at the border looking across into China. We were no exception. My claim was, and still is, that with an adroit leg maneuver, I actually put one foot over to stand on Chinese soil. That was an achievement in those days—setting foot in China!

Some people are just naturally skeptical—even when a good story is true!

They did believe another story when we arrived at the Panama Canal. I could produce an old newspaper clipping to prove it. As the youngest person ever licensed by the State of California to be a telegraph operator, I had been on one of the first ships to go through the canal after it was completed.

Memories that went back beyond half a century were with me as the Rotterdam crossed from the Pacific to the Atlantic through what stands to this day as one of the world's engineering marvels.

Setting a Date

When we arrived back in Connecticut late in April of 1969, there was no question in my mind about proceeding with the planned retirement. Everything had gone beautifully at Echlin. I was confident this would continue to be the case.

Fred was pleased with our negotiations in South Africa and asked whether Beryl and I would be willing to return there later in the year to complete the arrangement with Charger. This was fine with us. We liked the country. We believed it held great opportunities for Echlin. And handling assignments of this kind could be a helpful way of staying at least to some extent involved.

As to actually stepping down as chairman, we had a board meeting scheduled for June 23. That would be an ideal time to make it official.

Although we were busy with a number of transition details leading up to that date, it was difficult for me to avoid reflecting on the six decades my working life had spanned, and on how far the automobile industry had come.

Just think of it. Only three years before I joined Earl in his repair shop in 1915, Charles Kettering's development of the self-starter did away with the crank. This provides an idea of how early in the history of the industry we entered it.

And the remarkable succession of improvements and refinements that accompanied the industry's growth as we grew with it. Excitement and fanfare greeted the announcement of each innovation down through the years. I kept thinking of some of them:

Balloon tires, as they were called when they appeared in the 1920s. "Air-cushioned" rides to get away from the bumping and jolting produced by the slim ones they replaced. How welcome they were! Then, years later, the tubeless tires eliminating bothersome inner tubes.

Starting with high-octane gasoline, the whole procession of contributions to improved engine performance, including our own products.

Better and safer braking systems—four-wheel brakes, hydraulic brakes, disc brakes, anti-locking devices—again, with our own products playing a prominent role in the progression.

Heaters for winter and vents for summer, leading to all-weather air conditioning. Antifreeze for cold weather, coolant for hot weather, evolving into all-weather fluid. Rugged new batteries to withstand the severity of any climate. Snow tires to replace constantly breaking chains. Directional signals that made it unnecessary to open windows and stretch out arms to indicate turns.

Free-wheeling and overdrives, followed by automatic transmissions that provided both. Front-wheel drives that facilitated driving in snow and made for more leg room in cars.

Power steering and power brakes to ease the task of driving. Power windows that automated their opening and closing.

All these were only part of a long and illustrious list. What marvelous accomplishments there had been over those six decades!

Making It Official

Everything went as planned at the June 23 board meeting. My resignation as chairman was accepted. Fred was elected to succeed me. As a reelected director, I was named chairman of the executive committee.

So, it wasn't the closing of a book by any means. A chapter had ended, but another was beginning. During the next several years, Echlin was to reach heights we couldn't possibly have envisioned in earlier days. Although my status had changed, I was to have the opportunity of still traveling along with it.

In my case, then, it was appropriate to put quotes around the word "retired." Even so, my colleagues had a retirement dinner for me.

It was a great affair. Long-familiar faces from all over the country. Lots of warm greetings and well wishes. Much happy reminiscing.

To look around the room that night was to see or think about individuals, many retired, who, starting years before, had played important roles in Echlin's progress and success. It would be virtually impossible to name all of them. Some appear in preceding pages of this story. Among others who either were present or came to mind were:

Harry Anderson, who joined us in 1944 on the production line. Harry advanced to draftsman, then became chief product engineer for electrical parts, moved up to executive positions, and ultimately was a group vice president heading our operations in the Southern Hemisphere.

Lloyd Bogart, who went to work in our Cleveland warehouse in 1933 and later had charge of it. Lloyd moved with us to New Haven in 1940, served as traffic manager, then as production manager, and before he resigned in 1946 to become a NAPA jobber, was an Echlin salesman in the Ohio territory.

Dubie Dubendorff. Dubie came to us as a salesman when we were still in San Francisco. After World War II, he was one of our regional managers. Some years after, he was appointed sales manager and soon was vice president in charge of sales. Ill health forced him to retire in 1965.

Henry Leonard. Henry had been with us since 1953, coming in as treasurer. He later became vice president as well as treasurer. All the years until his retirement, he handled our financial affairs in a most capable manner and was a greatly respected officer of the company.

John Leslie. Johnny had been sales manager for Gilfillan Brothers in their Kansas City branch. He joined us early in 1929 and compiled our first ignition catalogue. He stayed in San Francisco as sales manager, then represented us in Southern California. With illness making it hard for him to travel, he came to New Haven in 1949 to head our catalogue department.

Elmer Lillie, whom I had known from the time we were night students at the Polytechnic School of Engineering. Elmer started with us in 1931 as a part-time salesman, then became full-time. He represented us in the Minneapolis territory, moved to Cleveland in charge of our warehouse, and on to New Haven. He headed our sales promotion when he retired in 1964.

Al Moeller. Al joined us the first year we were in New Haven. He started in the sales department, handling the vital job of customer relations and doing it extraordinarily well. Al progressed in the company. At the time of the dinner, he was manager of our electrical parts products.

Barney Niedt. Barney was our customer service manager after he joined us in 1935. In 1940, he shifted to our Pacific Coast sales staff, becoming regional manager for that territory and Hawaii in 1953. Barney made an outstanding mark with clinics he conducted for thousands of automotive men. He retired in 1965.

Stan Peden, who began with us as a salesman in northern California in the 1930s. In 1946, Stan became our first actual sales manager. Until then, I had been in direct charge of sales myself. He did a great job in this capacity, spending at least three-fourths of his time traveling throughout the United States.

Earl Sambrook. On a trip east in 1939, I met Earl and was impressed with his qualifications. He came with us as a salesman in the New York territory, showed broad capability, and in 1945 became manager of our plant in New Haven. In 1949, he was made vice president in charge of production.

Gordon Shove. Gordon came to us when we moved to New Haven in 1940. He served as foreman of our contact production for many years. An excellent production man, he helped organize departments at our other plants and performed many other special assignments for the company.

Burt Sibley. One of our first new employees in New Haven, Burt began as shipping clerk. He was advanced to purchasing agent when we moved to the Branford plant. Burt later became our materials manager, a job that was growing in its complexity, and handled it in a highly capable manner.

George (Simmie) Simmons. Simmie was with the NAPA warehouse in Boston. In 1935, we made an agreement with him to work part of his time for Echlin as a salesman in the New England territory. He joined us full-time in 1940, was sent to the Atlanta area for a time, then back to New England. Simmie retired in 1962 to start his own business.

Joe Volz. Joe had been with us since 1930. He was in our Cleveland warehouse for a number of years and came to New Haven in 1940. He was made foreman of our bakelite molding department, a job he handled so well he later became factory superintendent.

Walt Walters, who joined us as a salesman in upstate New

York in 1940. Walt moved to New Haven in 1946 to become purchasing agent for our plant. He went on from this to perform the skilled function of heading our ignition technical services.

People. These individuals and countless others—in the plants, in our offices, on the road as salesmen, in varied other capacities—were the ones who had built Echlin. How proud I was of them and of what, working together, we had been able to accomplish.

The New Chapter

Chapter 9
The New Chapter

A Quick Adjustment

Beryl often said that my "retirement" amounted to a mere transfer of office from the plant in Branford to our home in Guilford a few miles away.

She had a point.

Our house at Sachem's Head in Guilford was on a slope directly overlooking Long Island Sound. We had built it a few years before, and it had been designed with a special room above the second floor. This, with windows running across the front to view the sound, was my office at home. Or, as friends used to say, my crow's nest.

It was a pleasant place to work, as I had found on many weekends, to say nothing of nights, when a brimming briefcase commanded attention.

During the days in New York preparing for Echlin's listing on the New York Stock Exchange, I had developed a fascination with the stock market. Echlin's favorable stock performance on the exchange over the six ensuing years heightened this fascination.

If I ever had the time to study the market and had a little capital to invest, I kept telling myself, this was a pursuit I would love to follow.

There was time now. And fortunately there was some capital. So, with no delay whatever, I occupied myself with this new interest.

All the information I began collecting on different companies and their stocks soon gave my crow's nest the appearance of a broker's office. But it was stimulating to read about them, to analyze them, and to devise my own system for charting them.

Closeness to John was a real plus in all this. As mentioned earlier, John had been with Echlin for a time and now was a director, but he had returned to his chosen profession of being a stockbroker. We had some interesting, and for me valuable, discussions once I began delving into the stock market as an amateur.

Meanwhile, there were telephone calls from Fred to find out how I was getting along and to tell me about things at the company. Also, reports and proposals arrived for study and comment. To this day, Fred has been extremely thoughtful and gracious about telephoning to keep me in touch with progress at Echlin.

So, adjustment to a changed pattern of life didn't prove difficult at all. I was in a new groove and enjoying it.

My involvement with the stock market is something I've found interesting ever since, luckily with good outcomes. It has been a satisfying complement to my serving on the board and in other endeavors with Echlin.

A Remarkable New Line

As for Echlin, more was going on than ever.

Sales were increasing faster than the overall automotive parts industry was growing. This was due to our gaining wider participation in the market by bringing new products into it.

An exciting example in 1969 was a new system of ignition parts—Echlin High Performance Ignition. This had been under development for some time, and we had great expectations for it. Specially engineered, but to be mass-produced, the line included a contact set, condenser, coil, distributor cap, and rotor.

The introduction of these new high performance products

was a dramatic one. Although it had occurred in February while we were on the cruise, we heard glowing and enthusiastic reports about it when we returned.

The locale had been the Daytona Beach, Florida, raceway. The nation's top stock car racers were competing there. A kit containing the new products was offered to the competitors in each race.

This turned out to be a master stroke of promotion by our people. Owners, drivers, and mechanics were so impressed with the improved engine performance the new products gave them that they not only used them there, but in later races elsewhere.

The word spread that Echlin had come up with a remarkable group of new ignition products. Not only were professional drivers talking about them, but of great importance to us, the word was getting to service station operators, garage owners, fleet maintenance men, and mechanics who could select them to repair their customers' cars.

In these high performance ignition parts was an excellent illustration of a policy long established as an Echlin hallmark. Echlin parts must be of a quality at least equal to, or preferably (and usually) better than the original parts they replace. By providing easier starting, greater reliability, and faster and smoother acceleration, the high performance ignition system represented a significant advance over original equipment parts.

The Import Market

Another particularly noteworthy development around that time was Echlin's entry into what rapidly was becoming an important segment of the total replacement parts market.

Analyses showed that the number of imported cars in the United States had climbed to six percent of all the passenger vehicles on our roads. Not only that, but one out of every 10 new cars being sold was a foreign model. Furthermore, there was every indication these figures would continue to rise.

Obviously, it would be smart for Echlin to get into this growing segment and take advantage of the potentials it offered.

Action was taken accordingly. The first step was our introduction of a complete range of Volkswagen repair parts to NAPA's distribution network. The line had excellent customer acceptance.

Only some of these parts were manufactured by Echlin. Most were imported from West Germany. We strengthened our position by acquiring the Unex Products Corporation of New York, importers of parts for Volkswagens.

We had, and followed, a two-part plan. One was to import parts for other foreign cars from the countries in which they were made. The second, and our real objective, was progressively to manufacture more of the parts ourselves.

Considering how sales of foreign cars have mushroomed over the years since, these were timely moves.

International Expansion

Beryl and I returned to South Africa in the fall of 1969 to work out final details of our acquiring a 50 percent interest in Charger. Everything went according to plan, with the Johannesburg company becoming Echlin Charger.

While we were there, we enjoyed another marvelous safari, and experienced again the wonderful hospitality of the Marcus family and others we met.

South Africa was an important part of an international market that was growing at a faster rate than was true in the United States. More than half of the world's automobiles now were in use outside of our country. The outlook was for this ratio to climb progressively beyond that point.

In 1970, the company succeeded in obtaining substantial holdings in two additional operations. One, which became Echlin Mexicana, was in Mexico City. The other, Manauto, was located in Valencia, Venezuela.

The following year, Berg Manufacturing Co. of Toronto, with facilities in Scotland and West Germany, was acquired. This brought us into the business of making and marketing air brake systems and replacement parts for heavy trucks.

Together with Echlin-United and Berg in Canada, these additions gave us production facilities in six nations outside of the United States. We were to have more as time went along.

Product Development

All of us were justly proud of another type of addition in 1971. It was Echlin's new product development laboratory.

Located in Hamden, Connecticut, this facility was established for two purposes. One was to strengthen our consistent program of improving existing products. The other was to accelerate our continuing program of developing top-quality new products.

All the equipment put into the laboratory was the very latest and most efficient available. The facility was recognized as the most modern installation of its kind on the East Coast.

With it, our product planning and engineering personnel could perform dynamic testing of products under actual vehicle operating conditions. This enabled them to make realistic evaluations of our electrical, ignition, and fuel system components.

One of the major pieces of equipment was a dynamometer that could be adjusted to simulate all types of driving conditions, from level road to hill climbing.

Another was a diagnostic console with meters that measured and reported electrical, ignition, and fuel system performance.

A third was an infrared gas analyzer. This was used to evaluate the efficiency of air-pollution control products designed for automobiles.

As in all competitive industries, the company that stays

ahead of the market is the one that is innovative in coming up with new products, while maintaining the integrity of its present products. Echlin had been able to do this. Our new laboratory was an investment in assuring that we would continue to do so.

Traveling Clinics

That same year, 1971, an important product was added to the Echlin High Performance Ignition System. This was an ignition distributor of advanced design.

The initial products in the high performance line had been received enthusiastically in the field. With the new distributor making the line complete, an aggressive program was launched to give it heavy marketing support.

The program featured an extensive series of night clinics among the more than 4300 NAPA auto parts jobbers and their garage and service station customers. These were conducted by highly trained Echlin specialists.

The clinics were designed to demonstrate how the products in the line could help the above customers to improve the quality and reliability of engine tune-ups. Motion pictures, slide presentations, and question and answer techniques were used not only to inform and illustrate, but also to dramatize the superior quality and performance of the products.

They were effective. They sold the merchandise. They created national awareness of the products and what they could do. They were another significant step in Echlin's sales outpacing the market.

The success of these demonstrations made me think back to my own early selling days after taking the Frank Beckman course. Don't just *tell* what your products can do; *show* what they can do. The technique had grown much more sophisticated. But it was the same basic technique. And it still worked.

One of the things that always has pleased me the most

about Echlin's reputation as an organization relates to our salesmen. They long have been regarded by customers everywhere as the best trained in the entire NAPA network of manufacturing companies.

The art of selling has been the heart of every sales-training program we have conducted, every sales meeting we have held. Combined with quality products, it has been the pivot of Echlin's success.

The Sun Beckons

The new life certainly was going well.

Echlin was doing splendidly under Fred's leadership. I couldn't have been more delighted with the great things the company was doing. And I was still fascinated with my new interest, the stock market, managing to stay in the desired column of the profit-and-loss ledger.

Not only was I managing to show a profit, but my involvement in the market provided one of the most rewarding experiences of my life.

We had several good friends who were widows. They needed advice with their investments and asked me to help. I began making suggestions which fortunately worked out well for them. This continued. They became known as "Jack's widows." I really derived a lot of warm pleasure from serving as their investment advisor and was so happy that their holdings kept rising in value.

Along the line, one of these ladies built a house in the Santa Cruz mountains in California. It always tickled me when we would visit there and she would say, "This is the house that Jack built."

In the winter of 1971, Beryl and I went to Florida. The weather was great. We found how pleasant it was to experience balmy days in midwinter, often with friends from the North who had come to the sun for vacations or to establish homes.

The more we enjoyed ourselves, the more we talked about

the advantages of moving there. Jet travel made Connecticut just a short distance away in terms of time. I still could be readily available for anything special that might come up. There would be no problem getting there for board meetings which we could combine with family visits, as well as with seeing friends.

With all these things in mind, we decided to look for a condominium. What luck we had! A handsome new apartment building had just been completed overlooking Lake Boca Raton, just a bit in from the ocean in Boca Raton. We immediately fell in love with it and bought an apartment with a lake and ocean view that never has lost its delight for us.

It was the first and only apartment we looked at. We moved to it later that year.

The room I use for an office is not a crow's nest per se. But it's the closest thing to it!

Jack with Mrs. Dorothy Pardo, his longtime secretary and a devoted and valuable employee.

One of several Sparky ads developed by the Humbert & Jones Advertising Agency in the late 1940s.
(Courtesy of *Jobber Topics*)

Introduced in 1949, the Visumatic program is still a vital inventory management tool for thousands of NAPA dealers.

Continued growth of the business necessitated construction
of these new quarters in Branford, Connecticut, in 1957.

Wilton Looney, who succeeded Carlyle Fraser as head of Genuine Parts Company in 1961, continued a close personal and business relationship with Jack Echlin.

Jack Echlin (center) confers with officials in 1963 as Echlin shares are traded on the New York Stock Exchange for the first time.

John Echlin Jr., who was instrumental in the establishment of
Echlin's Canadian plant in the mid-1960s.

Fred Mancheski joined Echlin in 1963 as vice president, manufacturing and engineering, and later was elected president. He was elected chairman and chief executive officer upon Jack Echlin's retirement in 1969.

Jack Echlin's involvement in the community included such activities as little league baseball team sponsorships.

Jack Echlin was a noted teacher and author on salesmanship. His techniques helped build a strong sales force for Echlin.

Jack's book on salesmanship was published in 1967, and is used today as a teaching guide.

Jack, atop a camel, on a stop in India during the Echlins' round-the-world tour in 1969.

Jack Echlin (L) and Fred Mancheski upon Jack's retirement
in June 1969.

Fred Mancheski congratulates Jack Echlin (R) upon Jack's induction into the Automotive Hall of Fame in 1985. He joined automotive pioneers like Henry Ford, Alfred P. Sloan, and Walter P. Chrysler.

Beryl and Jack Echlin enjoy a shoreline setting in Branford, Connecticut, at the Pine Orchard Yacht and Country Club.

Echlin built this new worldwide headquarters building at historic Double Beach in Branford, Connecticut, and has occupied it since the fall of 1981.

The past and the future are contrasted by the large 1950s mechanical voltage regulator and the modern 1980s electronic version. These parts represent the wide variety of manufacturing expertise which Echlin has developed.

Beryl Echlin at the New York Stock Exchange, where Echlin Inc.'s board of directors met in June 1988 to celebrate the 25th anniversary of the company's listing. Mrs. Echlin was elected an honorary director.

An Eventful Era

Chapter 10
An Eventful Era

Always Ahead

As only a board member rather than both a board member and a manager, I could look at Echlin from a somewhat different vantage point. And I surely liked what I saw as the company moved ahead in the early 1970s.

Advances were occurring rapidly in the automotive industry. Echlin was playing a vital and prominent role in them. Our people were assuring the company's continuous growth through consistently demonstrating outstanding ability to do four crucial things: anticipate, plan, prepare, and execute.

To recall a number of developments in the year 1972 alone is to appreciate how true this was. Much was happening. Much was on the horizon. Echlin was in the vanguard on all fronts.

Even after all those years, it was exciting to watch and, though in a different way, to still be a part of it.

An Ingenious Device

A wave of public and governmental pressures to curb air pollution from cars had risen across the nation. This stemmed from the mounting concern for the environment that was being expressed and evidenced in a variety of ways.

California had adopted a law requiring emission reduction equipment on all passenger cars that had been manufactured beginning in 1966 and running through 1970. Other states were bound to follow suit.

After two years of research, development, and testing in
our own as well as independent laboratories, plus 270,000
miles of actual road testing, Echlin was ready in 1972 with
an automotive pollution control system. It was one of two
approved by the California Air Resources Board.

The heart of our system was a marvelous little sonic
generator that created ultrasonic energy. When this high
energy entered the air-fuel mix, it had an immediate effect
on the fuel mixture, making it finer, dispersing it better. The
result was more efficient and complete burning of gasoline
within the engine.

Emissions of oxides of nitrogen were cut up to 52 percent.
Unburned gasoline (hydrocarbons) showed reductions as
high as 42 percent. Carbon monoxide was reduced as much
as 31 percent. No other system that had been developed
could achieve such major reductions.

Skill and thoroughness on the part of our technicians had
produced a superior device. Echlin was poised to gain important market share in this new category of automotive
parts.

Adapting to Change

The company also was displaying versatility in the face of
change affecting some of its traditional products.

Use of electronics in ignition systems was increasing. So
much so that in 1972 one major automobile manufacturer
standardized on electronic ignition. While such Echlin products as ignition coils and distributor caps remained as component parts of the new systems, the company's conventional contact sets and condensers did not.

Our people had recognized the growing role of electronics.
They had designed needed replacement parts for the new
ignition systems and had tooled to manufacture them.

This transition to electronic ignition had an interesting
balancing-out aspect.

One of the advantages it offered was extended service life.

This naturally would reduce the frequency of parts replacement; in other words, it could have significant implications for us in terms of volume. On the other hand, the new electronic parts were as much as 10 times more expensive than conventional components. So, on balar ce, we figured that any adverse effect on numbers would be more than offset by a favorable effect on dollars.

New, Safer Brakes

With greater highway safety a constantly sought national objective, and with disc brakes providing safer braking systems, disc brakes had become standard front-wheel equipment on most cars being produced in the United States.

There was every likelihood that within the ensuing five years, many cars also would have them on the rear wheels, and that this increasingly would be the case.

Our Brake Parts Company had a full line of disc brake parts for passenger cars and light trucks. With continuous advances in view, Echlin had design and product groups at work to insure the company's full participation in this growing market.

But what we were doing in the area of safer brakes didn't stop there.

In 1972, Berg Manufacturing Company, our air brake subsidiary, introduced a new, advanced anti-skid system for heavy trucks. This was especially timely in view of new federal regulations, to take effect in 1974, requiring that large trucks, buses, and tractor trailers be able to stop in a straight line on wet or dry roads at specified speeds and loads.

The Berg system was electronic. Developed in Europe by Fiat, Echlin was licensed to produce and market it in the United States.

Here again, ingenuity had been at work to deliver an effective means of meeting a need. A sensor on each wheel of the truck combined with a small computer to translate wheel-speed information into air-pressure pulses. These, in turn, created an automatic process of brake releasing and reapplying. The brakes were prevented from locking the wheels while the vehicle was in motion. Hence, skids were avoided.

The following year, the Department of Transportation set forth further requirements. These called for a dual split braking system on both truck tractors and trailers. The objective was to ensure full brake capacity if half the system should fail.

Berg engineering and manufacturing personnel designed all the new products needed to meet these requirements. In the middle of 1973, the company was the first to offer the total safety package to the trucking industry.

Added Countries

Our international operations also were on the march.

In 1972, Brazil became the second country in South America in which we had a manufacturing facility. This resulted from our purchase of Auto Pecas Henrique Schenk in San Paulo.

Schenk was highly regarded throughout Brazil. The firm manufactured electrical parts for cars and trucks. These, known as the HS brand, were sold to manufacturers of new vehicles as well as to the replacement parts market. With the acquisition, equipment was installed to produce our ignition parts. All HS brand products became HS-Echlin.

The automotive population was growing faster in Brazil than anywhere else in the world in the early 1970s. Prospects were bright for this newest member of our growing international network.

It was a network that had its largest single addition in 1973. This came with the purchase of Park Brothers in England.

Park was the company Beryl and I had visited a few years before. It was a well-established firm and gave us the kind of presence we wanted in England. All of us were delighted when an agreement was signed. We felt it also would give us a base from which to build and expand in the European Common Market.

But, as will be seen, we were in for later disappointment.

A Year To Remember

Echlin reached a milestone in 1973. And it seemed mighty impressive at the time.

That year, Echlin's sales climbed above $100,000,000. Actual volume was $125,661,000.

When that figure was announced, I remember getting out my 21-inch slide rule. My calculations showed this volume was 1047 times the $120,000 break-even mark we celebrated reaching in 1925!

To digress for a moment, mentioning that 21-inch slide rule brings back some amusing memories.

At the Polytechnic School of Engineering those long years ago, how to use a slide rule was one of the first things we learned. I had carried a pocket one around with me ever since and found it a surprisingly handy thing to have for all kinds of purposes. But the big one. That was something!

Al Moeller often tells how he and another man on the staff would help me "price by slide rule." With some 2500 items in five pricing categories to consider, we would go through the product lines. The slide rule told us what we needed to know about figures relating to costs, margins, and other factors that went into price determination.

For me, it put some fun into a tedious job. I'm not sure the others got that much fun out of it. And I don't suppose it was a method in common use by other companies.

And that big slide rule was a fixture in my office. Whenever a proposal or idea was being presented for my approval, I'm told there always was a good deal of shuddering the instant I got out that formidable instrument and began doing some calculating. It often saved us money, however.

But getting back to that $125,661,000, there was a significant thing about our steady climb in volume.

On an average, our sales had doubled every four years since 1959 when we first sold our stock in the over-the-counter market. Two-thirds of this growth had come from increased volume in our basic product lines, and one-third from acquisitions. This is a pattern that has continued.

Wise Moves

Speaking of acquisitions, results were showing that Fred had negotiated two excellent domestic additions in 1970. One was Ace Electric Company in Kansas City, Missouri. The other, an Ace subsidiary, was Jameson Parts Manufacturing Company in Van Nuys, California.

With Ace, Echlin got into the manufacturing and marketing of repair parts for alternators, generators, and starters, an expanding business. A well-known line of replacement parts for automotive clutches came with Jameson.

In 1973, Ace moved into a new manufacturing facility. This was needed to meet rising demand for its parts from the rebuilding trade. The same year, Jameson occupied a new building in Chatsworth, California, to handle the increased volume of clutch parts the market required.

Two other businesses acquired in 1973 proved to be equally wise investments.

From the Weber Tool Company came a line of high performance clutches, together with a line of high performance engine flywheels and related parts.

With the purchase of Lift Parts Manufacturing Company, Echlin entered into distributing a broad range of service repair parts for fork lift trucks. Lift Parts, based in Des Plaines, Illinois, sold its products to a network of independent sales and service outlets specializing in lift truck parts. It provided us with a new market and new product line that fit nicely into our overall manufacturing pattern, and opened additional opportunities for growth.

More Pleasant Assignments

From the time of our two visits to South Africa in 1969, I had taken a special interest in Echlin Charger's progress there.

During 1973, Charger expanded its facilities for manufacturing Echlin ignition parts. Also, it began initial marketing of brake parts under the Echlin-United brand name. In addition, the company established a marketing arm to handle products from Ace Electric in the United States and from Park in England.

With all this activity, and because I had maintained such a close interest in the developments, Fred asked Beryl and me about the possibility of making another trip to Johannesburg. This was in 1974. Delighted with the opportunity of going to that country again, we quickly agreed with the idea.

Since it would be convenient to do so on the way back, Fred suggested further that we visit the Berg operation in West Germany. Much also was going on there, and it always is beneficial for the home office to have firsthand observations.

And with Berg's anti-skid system for heavy trucks having been developed by Fiat, and our being licensed by that company to produce it in the United States, a visit with the Fiat people in Italy could be part of the itinerary.

It all sounded interesting and appealing to us. So, late in the summer of that year, off we went.

A Quality Operation

As brought out earlier in connection with our first negotiations in 1969, Charger's basic work had been the rebuilding of starters, alternators, and generators. Adding Echlin ignition parts to its production and marketing had been a profitable move. We were confident the same would hold true with the other additions that were in progress.

Viewing the expanded and still-expanding operations firsthand and studying the sales charts confirmed that confidence.

Cecil Stewart, who had been sales manager for the Marcus brothers when they fully owned the company, and who had been made general manager when it became an Echlin subsidiary, now had the title of managing director. We had been impressed with him at the outset and continued to be. Extremely capable and a hard worker, he was dedicated to quality in production and had excellent marketing instincts.

We spent a good deal of time analyzing market potentials and ways and means of merchandising and selling our different product lines. Everything about the picture was most encouraging, and I knew Fred and the other directors would be pleased with the report I would carry back.

Cecil and his wife June made us feel warmly welcome throughout our stay and entertained us graciously. We formed a close friendship with them. On trips to the United States, they have visited us many times in Florida. It always has been such a pleasure to see them.

Although business was our primary purpose in being there, and we did tend to that first, Beryl and I enjoyed going on another safari, this time in Kenya. And this time our fascination also led us to an interesting trip into Tanzania.

A Firm Hand

Our Berg operation in Walldorf, West Germany, near Heidelberg, was headed by Mrs. Gisela Schleweis. Gisela was an extremely smart and capable woman. She managed with precision and decisiveness. She had answers to questions and could support them with facts.

We covered a lot of ground in our discussions. We examined present production and capabilities of expanding production. We reviewed market potentials. We talked selling. Gisela was responsive to thoughts and ideas I passed along. I was impressed with hers and assured her they would be taken back to Connecticut.

We stayed at a hotel in Heidelberg. Nearby was a castle with a courtyard. It was just as Sigmund Romberg had

portrayed that storied German city in "The Student Prince."
And what do you think?

We saw "The Student Prince" performed in the courtyard
of that castle. It was an enchanting evening we've never
forgotten. Our trip to Heidelberg was complete!

Speaking of Cars . . .

From Heidelberg we traveled to Milan in Italy. Greeting us
at the airport were Sergio Campanini and his wife, and
Sergio's mother and father. Sergio, who had married an
American girl, was manager of our Berg plant in Iola, Kansas.
He and his wife were in Italy visiting his family.

The car in which they met us was a 12-year-old handmade
Lancia owned by Mr. Campanini Sr. What an automobile! We
rode in it to Florence.

Sergio had anticipated how intrigued I would be with that
vehicle. Before we went to Florence, he and his father
had guided me on a full inspection of it at the beautiful
Campanini farm outside of Milan.

The Campaninis were a lovely family. They were marvelous
to us. Being with them was a delightful way to be welcomed
to Italy and to see some of the many sights for which that
country is so famous.

Sergio, our wives, and I went to Turin for a visit at the Fiat
plant and dinner with the president and three other
company executives.

The table at dinner had an interesting and unique
centerpiece. In a circle was a miniature of each model of car
Fiat had produced from the time it was founded. These were
for us. Our wives divided them. Back in America they were
conversation-piece mementos of our visit.

Fiat always has had an excellent reputation in the automotive industry. Seeing their production and development
facilities made it easy to understand why. Echlin had a fine
relationship with them through the anti-skid brake licensing
agreement. It was a pleasure to get to know the company
and the personable, highly talented people who ran it.

Another Highlight

Beryl and I always had wanted to see Scotland. This trip provided a good opportunity to do so. We flew to Glasgow where we had a rental car and driver waiting for us.

The driver was an Irishman with a Scotch accent, a combination that proved to be charming and entertaining. And he really knew Scotland.

We saw firths and lochs, glens and moors, highlands and lowlands. We watched Scotsmen, clad in colorful kilts, playing bagpipes. We visited the great University of Edinburgh, even stopped to view castles. And our driver especially enjoyed pointing out, with clear overtones of suggestion that we go in to see them, the homes of different brands of that most familiar of all Scotch products, whiskey.

In mentioning the one distillery we did visit, with no need for persuasion from our driver, I should set a bit of background.

It had come to be pretty well known among colleagues and friends that Scotch was my drink. Not that I consumed that much, of course; just that whenever there was occasion to have a drink or two, Scotch was for me.

Wilton Looney, although not an imbiber himself, was well aware of this liking. Thoughtful friend that he always has been, he somehow found out about a Scotch that must have inspired the term "pure nectar." It was called Glenfiddich. Not then available in America, he procured a bottle of it for me in Scotland.

From that time on, nothing could surpass Glenfiddich as far as I was concerned. When it did come on the market in the United States, I'm sure I was one of the first customers.

Now, back to our tour of Scotland. It was when we saw the sign "Glenfiddich" on a distillery building that there was no doubt in my mind about stopping. We were rewarded with seeing how that superb product was made by time-honored methods—and with a wee bit of a nip.

Scotland is a noble country!

Enter Electronics

Back home, Echlin was continuing to move forward by staying ahead of important developments in the automotive industry.

Among trends with particular significance for the company was the rapidly expanding use of electronic ignition systems, just as our people had anticipated.

Chrysler had introduced an electronic system for its 1973 model cars. General Motors and Ford installed their own in 1974 models. While the systems differed considerably in design, this meant that the vast majority of new American cars being sold had some form of electronic ignition.

From the time the Chrysler system was introduced, Echlin had been manufacturing and marketing replacement parts for it. Knowing General Motors and Ford were coming out with theirs, our engineers and technicians had performed the design, engineering, and production tooling needed for making replacement components.

But that wasn't all.

Electronic ignition was demonstrating clear and desirable advantages—more dependable starting even in adverse weather, smoother-operating engines for longer periods. It was correctly sensed that as word spread about these advantages, owners of prestandard-equipped models would want it on their cars.

Echlin developed a retrofit electronic ignition conversion kit accordingly. First offered in the middle part of 1974, the kit made it possible to install the new type of ignition on most eight-cylinder cars dating back to 1958. A similar kit for six-cylinder cars was in process.

What made Echlin's prominence in this work especially significant financially was the much greater price of parts for electronic systems. Experiences indicated that while some reduction in unit sales was involved, a 350 percent increase in dollar volume of sales could be realized.

Furthermore, every sign pointed to a massive increase in

the use of electronics in additional ways for automobiles. The expertise Echlin was gaining in its work with electronic ignition could prove invaluable in designing, producing, and selling replacement parts for whatever types of automotive electronic systems that might evolve.

More Acquisitions

In terms of volume, 1976 turned out to be another milestone year for Echlin. Sales passed the $200,000,000 mark. But large figures were becoming so common at the company that I wasn't tempted to get out my slide rule again!

Three companies acquired that year and another in 1977 continued to broaden our production and marketing base. They were:

Peerless Instrument Company located in Niles, Illinois. Peerless manufactured engine tune-up and diagnostic equipment for professional mechanics and the do-it-yourself trade. Its sales were strong. We expected a good return from this addition.

Roto-Master, Inc. in North Hollywood, California. This firm produced diesel engine turbochargers and parts for turbochargers. The company, established in 1970, was a young enterprise with a promising future.

Kravex Manufacturing Corporation of Miami, Florida, a producer of automotive wire and cable. Kravex, with annual sales of about $10 million, offered good growth potential.

Tekonsha Engineering Company, Tekonsha, Michigan, which manufactured controls for electric trailer brakes. These controls were sold primarily to the growing recreational vehicle market.

So, while our products continued to be centered in the automotive parts field, Echlin progressively was diversifying its participation in that market.

A Disappointment

A difficult and unavoidable decision had to be made in 1978.

Our Park Brothers subsidiary in England, which all of us were so pleased to see Echlin acquire five years before, had not been doing well. We were sustaining losses from it and had to take some action.

Part of the problem could be attributed to adverse economic conditions. In addition, there were persistent labor problems. On top of everything else, a damaging fire had occurred at the plant.

After a thorough analysis, it was concluded that only a large injection of capital held any hope of making the operation profitable again. And even that could not be a certainty.

The only practical course was to halt our losses and liquidate the subsidiary.

While it was a sad day for all concerned when this happened, Beryl and I felt especially sorry about it. We remembered our pleasant visit to England in 1967, the prosperous concern Park was at that time, and the wonderful hospitality extended us by the Park brothers and their families.

But long ago I had learned that overcoming setbacks is part and parcel of keeping a company going forward. In the case of Park, this was precisely what our people did by pursuing other means of maintaining and expanding our European business.

Meanwhile, a happier note was being sounded in another part of the world. Our business in Australia was increasing rapidly. To handle it, we opened a distribution facility in Melbourne, Echlin Australia (Pty.) Ltd. The car population was rising in that dynamic country. We wanted to make sure our sales would keep rising with it. Being able to distribute parts more quickly was a key.

A New Field

Another step the company took in 1978 had positive and exciting long-term implications for Echlin. This was the establishing of the Sensor Engineering Company as a subsidiary. Its purpose was to develop commercially a highly advanced magnetic pulse-generating technology known as the Wiegand Effect.

Some two years before, we had been searching for a more effective ignition trigger. In this search, our people learned about an invention by John Wiegand, an engineer. He immediately was contacted, his invention was tested, talks were held with him, and Echlin obtained worldwide rights to the technology.

With wide uses foreseen for it, the Wiegand Effect was viewed as a major breakthrough in generating pulsed signals.

The technology is centered in a short length of fine alloy wire. This has an inner core and outer shell with different magnetic properties. In the presence of a small, permanent magnet, the polarity of the inner core snaps into alignment with that of the outer shell, generating a pulse of electricity in a sensing coil.

The pulse is stronger and more clearly defined than those offered by other known means. Among its advantages are that it operates without the input of electrical energy and is effective over an extreme range of temperatures.

The Wiegand Effect proved to be a superior ignition trigger when it was introduced in our high performance ignition system. But a multitude of other applications could be visualized for it. For example:

Security access at hotels, office buildings, factories, and other locations. Wiegand wires embedded in plastic cards produce pulse patterns exceedingly difficult to counterfeit. Echlin successfully has marketed these cards.

Motor vehicles. Already, of course, we had adopted it in our ignitions. Other promising applications could be a crankshaft speed and position sensor that would control ignition timing and fuel mixture, and a speed sensor that could be used in transmission controls or for speedometers, eliminating speedometer cables.

Industrial. Flow metering, for instance, where pulses from

wires mounted on a drum measure such things as gallons of water, chemicals, or gasoline delivered. And machine tool control, where signals from Wiegand wires can start or stop many kinds of operations.

Product development of this kind can be slow and costly. Our work with the Wiegand Effect has run true to this norm in a number of respects.

But, over the long run, the enthusiasm of our technicians and the confidence of our management can make our Sensor Engineering Company subsidiary one of Echlin's greatest assets.

On To Higher Pinnacles

Chapter 11
On To Higher Pinnacles

Continuing Assignments

On several occasions in the late 1970s, Beryl and I, at Fred's request, took additional trips for the company.

One was another visit to Johannesburg, which we were delighted, as always, to make.

The picture at Echlin Charger was bright. There were consistent increases in sales and net income. As managing director, Cecil Stewart was doing a superb job. We were pleased with the progress that had been made and encouraged by the outlook for further growth in volume.

One of the things I liked to do was accompany salesmen in calling on existing and prospective customers. It was a way of keeping in touch with the real world of selling products. I could observe how our salesmen were practicing the techniques that had been central to our growth over those many years. And I could give myself some testing to make sure I hadn't lost the touch.

To come right down to it, I guess it was just a case of never having lost the enjoyment of going out and selling Echlin products. Once Frank Beckman had taught me how to do it in those early San Francisco days, I forever had been a salesman at heart.

Also, we spent some time in Puerto Rico on other trips. The company had established a subsidiary in Ponce, Echlin of Puerto Rico, Inc.

Whenever we were there, we reminisced about the plant

dedication ceremony and "Papa Echlin." The governor, the Catholic bishop, the parish priest, and the mayor of Ponce were on hand to speak. And since we saw important potential for the Puerto Rican operation, our directors had flown down for the occasion.

All of the Puerto Rican dignitaries spoke in Spanish. It was clear they were addressing their remarks mainly to the plant manager and a small group of attentive individuals we had hired as our initial employees. At points in their talks, the speakers would turn, look at me, and make reference to "Papa Echlin."

Since these were the only two words we understood, what they were saying about "Papa Echlin" was a mystery. Somehow I got the impression "Papa" was promising all of them something, and I was getting a bit concerned about what it might be!

Then, when the speeches were over and we learned what had been said in Spanish, everyone was happy and I was relieved. We had set certain standards for the employees to meet in product quality and volume over a three-month period. We had told them that if these objectives were met, production would be expanded. That, of course, would mean more jobs.

What the speakers had been saying to the employees was that if they achieved the goals, relatives would be hired, too. So, "Papa Echlin" (I was singled out because of my name) would have a fine family of brothers and sisters working in the plant.

The family idea was an obvious incentive. Those first employees took only three weeks, not three months, to prove their capabilities. More jobs indeed were provided. And the facility became a great asset for the company.

Here, too, was a land we enjoyed. While it had a different basic culture from ours, its ties to America were everywhere in evidence. Calling on customers there was little different from doing so at home—and the fundamentals of selling applied in the same ways.

Speaking of calling on customers at home, we also spent time in the Midwest, a good deal of it in Kansas. Our Independence operation dated a long way back and I always had a special affinity for it.

So, although I was "retired," it was great to still have a hand in what was going on out in the territories.

Portrait of Progress

As the decade of the 1970s closed, Echlin had been a publicly held company for 20 years. Where did we stand? How had our stockholders fared? It was enlightening to take an inside look.

Our sales had reached $304,000,000 a year. They had increased at a compound rate of almost 20 percent annually. Since Fred had been at the helm more than half of the 20-year period and was due the large measure of praise for this record, I feel free to call it remarkable.

Over the 20 years, growth in net income had kept close pace with sales. It had run at a rate of 18.5 percent per year. In other words, growth had not been achieved at the expense of profits.

Dividends had been increased 19 times at a compound rate of 15.4 percent a year, and there had been five stock splits.

Anyone who bought 100 shares of Echlin common stock in 1959 and held them, owned 2400 shares in 1979. If, as cash dividends were received, the money was reinvested in more shares, the owner now had an additional 1569 shares. Combined, these shares were worth $65,000 on an original investment of $1650.

Only through a deep sense of responsibility to three groups can a company grow and prosper. These are its customers, its employees, and its stockholders.

We felt we could be justly proud of Echlin's record with all three of these groups.

Talk About Growth!

Early in the new decade of the 1980s, Echlin entered a period of unprecedented expansion.

This began in 1981 with the largest acquisition in the company's history: purchase of the Borg-Warner Automotive Parts Division.

Borg-Warner, one of the most familiar names in the automotive industry, long has been highly respected for product quality and integrity. Echlin's long-term agreement with the company provided the exclusive right to use the Borg-Warner trademark in the automotive aftermarket.

With the purchase, Echlin obtained two major manufacturing and distribution segments within the Borg-Warner Automotive Parts Division.

A Ballwin-Washington segment included two plants. One, in Ballwin, Missouri, performed all packaging, warehousing, and distribution. The other, in Washington, Missouri, manufactured an extensive variety of precision carburetor parts and emission control devices.

An Ottawa segment, operating in a modern plant at Ottawa, Illinois, produced rebuilt clutches for heavy duty vehicles and passenger cars. These were assembled similarly to new clutches and were regarded as meeting the highest standard of quality.

Along with these facilities, the purchase brought to Echlin a sales and distribution organization headquartered in Franklin Park, Illinois. This was supplemented by an export sales organization, also at Franklin Park, which served world automotive replacement parts markets. In addition, there were distribution operations in Canada, Puerto Rico, and West Germany.

The acquisition placed Echlin in new product areas that not only complemented its own, but which had immense potential for growth. Hence, it provided our company with new and wider opportunities to expand domestically and worldwide.

Rounding Out

Blackstone Manufacturing Co., Inc., located in Chicago, was another of the acquisitions that year.

Although a relatively small company, Blackstone manufactured a broad line of fuel pumps. Echlin carried a number of fuel system products—carburetor parts, emission control devices, and turbochargers for gasoline and diesel engines. Adding fuel pumps represented a further rounding out of our participation in fuel system production and marketing.

The Blackstone products had two characteristics that especially appealed to us.

One was their construction. The fuel pumps looked, fitted, and functioned the same as original pumps. Customers easily recognized them as exact replacements. The other characteristic was their quality. They were fully acceptable to automobile manufacturers as fill-ins for those they did not produce themselves.

With quality products and good relationships with customers, Blackstone provided Echlin with an excellent base from which to build increased volume in this field.

Joining Forces

Another of the acquisitions was M. Black Manufacturing Company of Philadelphia, a manufacturer of automotive ignition wire and battery cable.

Our Kravex subsidiary in Miami manufactured a similar line of products. Our strategy was to sell the property occupied by Kravex, move that operation to Philadelphia, and combine the best expertise of the two companies.

This was accomplished. The combined operation became Kravex Manufacturing Corp., based in Philadelphia.

The fourth acquisition in 1981, Mechanex Inc., located in Englewood, Colorado, also enabled us to do some combining.

Mechanex manufactured a unique, heavy duty wheel oil seal sold under the brand name of Barrier Seal. Its patented two-piece rubber construction did a superior job of sealing by conforming to the wheel hub and making allowances for any imperfections in the wheel. It could be removed and replaced easily with the wheel in an upright position and without pounding on the bearings, saving the mechanic up to 20 minutes in the process.

Wheel oil seals were used on the same heavy duty trucks, trailers, and other large vehicles that used our Berg Manufacturing Company air brake products. They normally were replaced when brakes were serviced. This meant that Berg and Mechanex were closely related from a product standpoint.

Since they had natural compatibility, we combined the Berg and Mechanex sales forces. Doing so provided each of the subsidiary companies with more representatives out in the field. These individuals, selling both lines, could concentrate on smaller territories, thereby performing a more thorough and complete job.

Because of their exclusive product features, Barrier Seals had been capturing an increasing share of the market. We looked to acceleration of this through our combined forces.

The following year, a further step was taken in this direction. Echlin acquired the Midland Brake Division of Midland-Ross Corporation, a well-known manufacturer of air brake products.

By combining the products of Berg and Midland, the company now had a complete line of air brake parts. Significantly, these included air compressors and valves necessary for installations on truck tractors.

A Christening

As Echlin had grown, so had its need for office personnel, space, and equipment. Although it had continued to serve as the headquarters location, we long ago had outgrown our office at the Branford plant. Many of our administrative functions had to be handled at scattered offices in the area.

It had been plain as we entered the 1980s that the company had to have a separate headquarters office building in which all the administrative work and equipment could be consolidated and housed.

It was clear also that any such building had to have sufficient space to allow for future expansion in the company's business.

The best answer was to design and build one of our own.

For this purpose, the company had purchased a several-acre piece of property on Long Island Sound. Located in Branford, the site was called Double Beach. The name came from the fact that a spit of land running out a short distance from the shore to a small island had sand and gentle slopes on both sides.

The property had been the site of a large hotel at the turn of the century. This was destroyed by fire in the early 1900s, and the land later was leased by a private club.

With a broad expanse of lawn reaching to the edge of a low cliff above the sound, the property has a swimming pool, tennis courts, picnic areas, easy access to the beach, and other amenities.

As a pleasant place for our employees to work, everything about it was ideal. And this certainly has proved to be the case. The recreational facilities are open to all our office and factory employees and their families. It always is a pleasure to see how many use them, how thoroughly they enjoy them.

Our new building was designed as a modern, functional structure with an exterior of Stony Creek granite quarried right there in Branford. It was completed in the fall of 1981.

A dedication ceremony was planned for June 27, 1982. Beryl was asked to perform the christening.

But this was to be no ordinary breaking of a bottle of champagne against one of the building's columns. Oh, my no! Instead, it was a bottle of water Fred had arranged to have taken from San Francisco Bay and shipped east.

That water Beryl splashed across one of the building's columns to christen Echlin's new corporate home had come from the same city and traveled to the same state that Echlin had 42 years before! Understandably, we were touched by Fred's memorable gesture.

Everybody was delighted with the building. After the ceremony and tour of the various departments and facilities, Beryl and I rested for a few minutes in an office that had been designated as mine whenever I might be in town.

How beautiful it was looking out across Long Island Sound, 42 years and 3000 miles from the new building we had been compelled to abandon in San Francisco.

Memories of how good those 42 years had been to Echlin gave way to visions of the future. For this lovely structure in which we were sitting was dedicated to Echlin's future, not its past.

Making the 500

The year 1983 was one of further consolidation of products among our subsidiaries. As well, some operations not performing up to profitability expectations were consolidated or eliminated. This is an inevitability from time to time for any company with such a broad range of lines.

But 1983 really is remembered for an exciting piece of news I received in Boca Raton in a telephone call from Fred.

Echlin had made the famous Fortune 500 directory of America's largest industrial companies!

Echlin in the Fortune 500! I could hardly believe it!

You might know that my regular copy of *Fortune* would be late in coming, this of all times! A friend and I scurried around to what I'm sure was every magazine stand in or anywhere in the vicinity of Boca Raton. It was late in coming this month, everybody said. As if I didn't know!

But, finally, it did arrive. Wow! There was Echlin, 457th on the list, with sales of $490,567,000 in 1982. We hadn't just barely made it. Forty-three companies on that list were behind us.

And that was only part of the story. We were all the way

up in 148th place in net income as a percent of sales. Even better, we were 79th in total return to investors.

You can believe I was in a hurry to telephone Fred with happy congratulations. Imagine thinking back in the J.J. Schnerr days that we'd ever reach a milestone of this kind!

What were we going to do for an encore? Climb higher on the list, of course!

A Broad Base

There was every reason to believe we would climb higher.

The market for vehicle replacement parts was growing steadily. Echlin consistently had performed ahead of the market. This had been accomplished by identifying and satisfying customers' needs through extending product lines, producing quality products, and paying close attention to service.

Continuous sharp focus on these policies assured uninterrupted growth for the company.

In this connection, it is relevant to review briefly the broad range of categories in which we now had products. This can be done by taking a quick look at the lineup as it stood in 1984:

For automobiles and light trucks: Electrical and electronic parts. Wire and cable. Hydraulic brake, fuel system, and power transmission parts. These and other products from Echlin divisions could be installed on the vast majority of cars and light trucks that were on the road. They were sold under such familiar brand names as NAPA Echlin, NAPA United, Ace, Auto-Tune, and Borg-Warner.

For heavy duty trucks and buses: A complete line of Midland/Berg air brake products that included air compressors, slack adjusters, gladhands, valves, and brake chambers. Ace parts for heavy duty starters. Roto-Master turbochargers. Fuel pumps. Wheel oil seals.

For off-road equipment: Turbochargers. Fuel pumps. Heavy duty electrical parts. These, manufactured by such Echlin divisions as Roto-Master and Ace, provided construction projects with ready replacements for earthmovers and other heavy equipment doing rugged work.

For industry: The company's Lift Parts subsidiary supplied a full line of parts for the materials-handling vehicles that had become so essential in factories, warehouses, and the like. These included drivelines, brakes, ignitions, electrical parts, and fuel system parts. Our Sensor Engineering Company's cards and readers employing the Wiegand Effect were in increasing use for security access and control.

For farms: Heavily worked farm tractors were using our Borg-Warner remanufactured clutches, Ace starter drive end housings, NAPA Echlin ignition parts, and our fuel pumps.

For recreational vehicles: Our ACCEL ignition parts were servicing motorcycles. Our Tekonsha Engineering Company was selling controllers for electric brakes to recreational vehicle distributors, as well as to manufacturers of small trailers, horse vans, travel trailers, and similar utility vehicles. Our Sierra Supply subsidiary was producing electrical and fuel parts for outboard engines.

For homes: Lawn mower parts. Fuel pumps. Carburetor repair parts. Other electrical parts. People needed all of these to maintain the several types of engine-powered tools and equipment that had become commonplace around the home. Echlin was supplying them.

Talk about a broad base! And the beauty of it was that our product lines were so compatible.

Joining Illustrious Company

A great and totally unexpected honor came to me in 1985. A communication arrived notifying me that I had been voted into the Automotive Hall of Fame.

What an overwhelming surprise! I hadn't even known I was being considered for it, and certainly hadn't expected to be.

The Automotive Hall of Fame was established at Midland, Michigan, in 1967. Its policy is to induct four individuals each year, two living, two deceased. The purpose was to honor and keep in memory those who have made significant contributions to the automotive industry.

Our dear friend and colleague Carlyle Fraser had been inducted posthumously in 1981. Past inductees included such industry pioneers as Henry Ford, Walter P. Chrysler, and Alfred P. Sloan, to name just a few.

Beryl and I were surprised and deeply warmed to see so many familiar faces at the induction ceremony in Midland on September 26. Our daughter Jane was there. John and his wife Sally. Fred and Didi Mancheski. Wilton and Martha Looney and several others who came with them from Genuine Parts. Our longtime friends Gene Muldoon, an Echlin director, and his wife May, and many others from Echlin.

James A. Ryder, founder of the Ryder truck rental firm, was the other living inductee. Edward G. Budd and Heinrich Nordhoff, the latter of Germany, were to be the two deceased new members.

Two thoughts kept running through my mind as we enjoyed the various festivities.

One was that I really was a representative receiving this honor. I was representing all the people who, down through the years, had made Echlin possible and whose work had built the company into the success it was.

Yes, Echlin had made significant contributions to the automotive industry. But they could not have come about without the dedication and ability of so many it had been my good fortune to have associated with me. It was my name that was going into the Hall of Fame. It had been their work that was placing it there.

My other recurring thought was that, as had been true with Carlyle Fraser's induction, this was recognition of the importance of replacement parts to the automotive industry.

Everybody knows who the automobile manufacturers are. But relatively few people think about the multitude of individual parts that go into those automobiles. Nor, until they are told by a repair shop or find out for themselves that they need them, do they think about parts to replace those that wear out.

Yet, without Echlin and other companies to manufacture replacement parts, without Genuine Parts and others to distribute them, without thousands of NAPA and other stores to sell them, automobiles could not keep running.

It was in recognition of this that my name, as Carlyle's had before me, went into the Automotive Hall of Fame on that festive September day of 1985.

Opening Opportunities

Meanwhile, Echlin's active, solid growth was maintained in the mid-1980s. Volume continued to expand with existing lines. Further important acquisitions were made.

Increasing its emphasis on brake parts, the company purchased the assets of the Brake Systems Division of Ray-mark. New and remanufactured drum brake shoes and disc brake pads produced by the division were widely known and respected under the brand names Raybestos and Grey-Rock.

Other actions were designed to build Echlin's presence and sales in the rapidly expanding European market.

One was the acquisition in 1984 of Graubremse in Heidelberg, West Germany, a manufacturer of air brake parts for medium and heavy duty vehicles in Europe.

Another was the purchase in 1985 of the Lipe Clutch Division of Lipe-Rollway Corporation in England. Lipe had won a well-deserved reputation as a producer of high-quality clutches, clutch components, and clutch assemblies for medium and heavy duty vehicles, as well as re-manufacturing clutches for those markets.

A third acquisition was Quinton Hazell, a British company manufacturing clutches, water pumps, steering and suspension system components, and other products for European and Japanese vehicles. This purchase in 1986 opened new overseas channels of distribution for Echlin in France, Italy, Germany, Belgium, and Holland.

An additional step involved Graubremse and Echlin's Berg subsidiary in the United Kingdom. In 1986, they entered into a joint venture with a British firm, Lucas Girling, to manufacture truck and trailer air actuation products and anti-lock brake systems for European distribution under the name of Grau Girling.

These actions in Europe established a major base for accomplishing two things. One, expanding our overall volume through selling more European-manufactured products. Two, developing European markets for Echlin products made in the United States.

Another Achievement

In 1986, Echlin had become a company with more than 12,000 employees manufacturing, assembling, packaging, and shipping more than 150,000 part numbers.

Having grown to this size, it was not surprising that in 1987 we reached another milestone. Our sales exceeded one billion dollars!

The actual figure was almost $1,100,000,000. I didn't need to get out the 21-inch slide rule to see that this volume was close to 10,000 times the $120,000 break-even point we were so elated about reaching in 1925!

That wasn't all.

When we made the Fortune 500 in 1983 as 457th on the list in annual volume, we said our encore would be to climb higher on the list. This we have done.

In 1988, Echlin moved into the Fortune 300.

What's more, there's absolutely no doubt in our minds about moving still higher.

Automated Quality

As volume has continued to grow, new production facilities have been opened and new equipment installed to meet the schedules. At the same time, we have introduced innovative methods of computerizing materials resource planning and production adjustments to achieve the greatest flexibility and efficiency possible. Too, we have adopted the latest types of automation wherever they have been applicable to our plants.

Our Branford factory is a striking symbol not only of the expansion we have undergone, but of sophisticated automation.

There have been so many additions to it that the plant now runs the full length of the property on which we put up our original structure in 1957. To enter from one end and look to the other is to observe what seems to be a mile-long sea of machines and busy workers.

On trips to Connecticut for board and other meetings, I like to stop by the plant for old times' sake whenever there is an opportunity to do so.

Some of our employees have been with us since we moved there, or even before that when we were in New Haven. It always is fun to visit with them, do some reminiscing about the old days, and hear about those little talks I used to make over the loudspeaker system from my office.

And, invariably, there are recollections about that uncanny business of walking through the factory and picking up, out of an entire lot, the one part that might have a slight imperfection. There was pandemonium then, but we can laugh about it now—and do.

A marvel today is the magic of new machinery that progressively has replaced what had been the most modern and efficient on the market at the time it was installed. Machinery that performs series of functions formerly done individually.

Our factory supervisors seem as uncanny now about anticipating things I want to know as I was those years ago about finding imperfections! They get right to the heart of the matter before I can even ask the questions.

Quality? By all means. They enjoy assuring me that those machines are designed to permit no margin of error in the quality of the components they forge. Then they get just as much enjoyment out of explaining the intricacies that make this possible. It's a good thing I took that night engineering course back in Oakland!

But even automation hasn't lessened the importance of *people* in a factory. Machines are marvelous instruments. Yet, they still need people around to do the thinking and to perform myriad other tasks.

In this context, my most recent conversations with workers in the Branford plant couldn't have tickled me more.

One, for example, with a young woman—she couldn't have been more than 22 or 23—who was checking a group of assemblies. I noticed how meticulous, but fast, she was. We exchanged a few words—I'm sure she didn't have the slightest idea of my connection with the company—and she held up one of the assemblies to me.

"Perfect!" she said. "The very finest."

What better words than those?

Then, there was a woman who had been with us for some time. She worked at an automatic wire-winding machine, applying long strips of tape at precise intervals. It was fast work and she was extremely facile with it. I complimented her.

She thanked me and added, "It's mighty important to have it exactly right every time. I make sure it is."

Good people are still fundamental to quality—even where high-precision machines are at work.

Always Progress

Among the wonderful things about the automotive business is the fact that it never is static.

One can look back and marvel at the dramatic improvements that have been made in motor vehicles over the years. At the same time, one can look into the future and see a procession of further improvements enhancing the pleasure, safety, and dependability of motor vehicle transportation.

This year—1988—I have been identified with the business for 73 years, almost three-quarters of a century. They have been exhilarating years because they have been spent in an industry that never has ceased to be exciting. And the future looks just as exciting as the past.

One of the especially interesting and significant developments on the horizon, for instance, is braking by wire.

Visualized are computer-directed wire impulses that will trigger air or hydraulic pressure to anti-lock brakes. The latter, of course, already are in use on considerable numbers of trucks and cars. They can be foreseen as one day becoming standard equipment on all new motor vehicles.

The quicker application braking by wire will achieve holds great promise for increased efficiency and safety. Progress in developing it will be watched with more than usual interest.

And assuredly coming are new devices for getting more efficient use of fuel. These will bring the triple benefits of lower operating costs, improved performance, and cleaner emissions.

Wide use of air suspension, with the smooth riding it will deliver, certainly is in the future picture. So are increasing numbers of cars with four-wheel drive and four-wheel steering.

These are but brief examples of advances, many not yet envisioned, that can be expected in an industry always seeking improvement.

With research consistently devoted to ahead-of-the-market development of new products and refinement of existing products, there can be no doubt about the contributions Echlin will make to the industry's continuing progress.

Across The Atlantic

Chapter 12
Across The Atlantic

An Expanding Market

For the past three years, I've watched with particular interest our progress in Europe. With what is occurring, great praise is due Fred Mancheski for his foresight and success in strengthening and building our presence there.

Much is being written and discussed in our country about the European Economic Community (EEC) and the goal of removing all trade barriers among its 12 member nations beginning in 1992. This naturally is capturing attention from American firms seeking to broaden and increase their European business. Echlin is in an excellent position to do so.

As can be seen from listing them, the 12 nations form an impressive network:

Belgium	Luxembourg
Denmark	Netherlands
France	Portugal
Greece	Spain
Ireland	United Kingdom
Italy	West Germany

However fully the trade barriers may be removed after 1992, one thing is apparent. The 12 nations are moving closer to becoming a single, internal market similar to the United States.

Add to this the planned completion in 1993 of the tunnel now being constructed under the English Channel between

England and France. The positive implications this long-hoped-for engineering feat holds for increased trade and economic development are enormous.

Emerging from all this activity is a combined market with 320,000,000 consumers and $4 trillion in purchasing power, the largest in the industrial world.

It is a market with immense potentials and opportunities for Echlin.

Our European volume in 1988 is running at a rate of about $200,000,000 a year. With the base our company now has there and with the aggressive steps being taken to expand it, this figure can be foreseen as more than doubling in the years immediately ahead and continuing to climb as the 21st century approaches.

Our Structure

As noted earlier, we acquired three European companies in the mid-1980s: Quinton Hazell and Lipe in England, and Graubremse in West Germany. Also, Graubremse and Berg, the European subsidiary we already had, entered into a joint venture with Lucas Industries to form Grau Girling, with Echlin holding 70 percent of the ownership.

All are grouped under Echlin Europe Inc. Roger Storey, managing director of this European group, has been with Echlin for some years. Along with Fred, he has done outstanding work in developing the combination of energetic enterprises we have there today.

To assess our position from three points of view is to draw strong confidence in what is ahead for us:

First, the extremely favorable outlook for motor vehicle growth in Europe.

Second, our European production facilities and products.

Third, our people there.

Growth Potentials

Figures I've studied show that in 1987 close to 12,400,000

cars, most of them built by their own manufacturers, were sold in Europe. This total was over a million more than were sold in North America, including imports.

It's plain that the European car market has become the largest in the world. And every sign points to its becoming larger. Analysts are predicting record sales through the 1990s.

One of the reasons for this prediction is the positive outlook for higher per capita car ownership.

According to the above-mentioned figures, Europeans presently own one car for every 2.7 people. This compares with North American ownership of one for every 1.8 people. With all that's happening, there's little doubt this gap will close.

We know that living standards already have reached high levels in many of the nations of the European Economic Community. Not only are they expected to continue to go up in those countries, but others in the group are on the move.

Much is stirring in Spain, for instance, with Portugal moving along, too. The Olympics are to be held in Barcelona in 1992. High-speed transit to and from France will make a long-term impact on trade. Spain is handling considerable production for the automotive industry, and its own per capita car ownership is climbing, as it is in Portugal.

Increased automobile ownership naturally goes along with rising living standards. More husbands and wives have separate cars. More young people get cars at earlier ages. These are patterns we know so well in our country, and they are being duplicated in Europe.

As will be seen a bit later when we take a quick look at our European facilities and products, Echlin is well-positioned for participating actively in this growth. This applies not only to the expanding aftermarket, but to gains we're making in supplying original equipment.

Turning to trucks, an equally bright picture comes into view for Echlin.

Many of the world's leading manufacturers of medium and heavy duty trucks, to say nothing of buses, are in Europe. They have earned justifiably great reputations for their vehicles.

Echlin's European companies are prominent in a number of areas of original equipment for these vehicles. A freer flow of goods among the 12 EEC nations will place heavier demands on the trucking industry. Along with growth for our original equipment products, a positive impact can be foreseen for the aftermarket.

Talk about potentials! Developments in Europe are presenting marvelous opportunities to us.

Broad Product Range

Quinton Hazell, with more than 1000 employees and some 2700 customers, is the largest of our European subsidiaries. Headquartered in England, the company also has operations in Wales, Ireland, Italy, France, and Belgium.

Its products are designed for European and Japanese cars and light trucks (the firm also has an office in Singapore). In addition, it manufactures components for tractors, commercial vehicles, and off-road applications.

The products—there are more than 30 all told—are in five categories: auto-electric, brakes, clutches, cooling equipment, and steering and suspension.

The company is noted for its extraordinary attention to quality control, so important to us and illustrating why we can look with confidence to our future in Europe. When I think of the engineering methods we used in the early days to assure quality, forever a top priority with us, how primitive they seem alongside of the amazingly sophisticated techniques of today. But they did the job then, when products were so much simpler.

Here are just three examples, among numerous others that could be cited, of how it's done at Quinton Hazell:

The company's clutch factory, one of the most advanced in Europe, was built purposely for integrated production that provides total control over the quality of every component.

Using the latest in endurance-testing techniques, every single aspect of clutch performance is analyzed constantly by subjecting samples to punishing wear and fatigue through simulation that is equal to thousands of miles of actual road travel. And to go a step further, a burst-test chamber is used to test sample clutches to destruction at revolution speeds far beyond the capacity of any automobile engine, just to make sure that quality is never compromised.

That's thoroughness!

As Britain's leading manufacturer of cooling system components, Quinton Hazell pioneered the use of die-cast aluminum bodies for replacement water pumps. Also, the company helped to develop the first pressed-steel impellers.

Virtually all of the body castings are produced at a state-of-the-art factory in North Wales. Quality is meticulously controlled through a series of advanced, multi-stage machining centers. And every single pump is tested individually for total reliability.

Here, then, we have not only another illustration of the quality factor always so important to us, but of being ahead of the market through research and innovation, also our hallmarks.

With its steering and suspension components, the company begins by testing the tensile strength of all raw materials that are used. Each batch must meet stringent standards. Then, in a fully integrated manufacturing facility, computer controls ensure precision across every stage of production. Before a single component is released for sale, samples from every production batch are tested through simulating a lifetime of stress and wear. Furthermore, parts in service continuously are checked for performance and wear.

It's not surprising that in the light of this strong focus on quality of replacement parts, Quinton Hazell has gained important original equipment contracts with European motor vehicle manufacturers.

Dual Goals

In my mind, anti-lock braking has been one of the most important developments during my lifetime in the automotive industry. Believing this, although I haven't been over to see firsthand its plant at Redditch in England, I've followed with deep interest the advances our Grau Girling joint venture has made in truck anti-lock braking systems.

In 1991, anti-lock brakes on trucks will be mandatory in many nations of Europe. The likelihood is that one day they will be mandatory the world over. The market position Grau Girling's achievements have won for it and the work it is doing on all-digital anti-lock systems for the 1990s stand this company at the forefront of what is ahead in this field.

From what I've learned about it, with some 40 engineers on the staff and with the very latest in high-tech equipment, the diagnostic work constantly going on in the Redditch plant can almost be likened to that in the most modern of medical laboratories. And it goes beyond the plant to intensive outside trials and tests under all conceivable driving conditions.

Maximum excellence is the objective and two things motivate the engineers' persistent pursuit of it.

One is the humanitarian goal of bringing greater safety to our highways.

The other is the commercial goal of benefiting from having the best products on the market to meet the need.

This search for the highest possible level of excellence is a further illustration of the premium our European operations place on quality. As we know from our long dedication to it, this is the most valuable ingredient that can go into any product.

Earlier I mentioned air suspension in connection with the future. This is expected to be the next major development in the European automotive industry. As they continue to perfect anti-lock braking, Grau Girling engineers also are working to assure that their company will be in the vanguard of what promises to be another exciting phase of automotive progress.

Meanwhile, at its other plant in Blackburn, Grau Girling, big in the trailer market, is producing top-quality air brake components and slack adjusters.

Clearly, this joint venture is proving to be a strong asset for Echlin.

Going for Growth

Lipe, our additional subsidiary in England, is an interesting operation.

It is known as the Rolls Royce of clutch manufacturers for medium and heavy duty vehicles. This applies similarly to clutches it produces as original equipment, and to those it remanufactures for the aftermarket.

Having built this reputation and having enjoyed good profits from living up to it, the company had been content to remain a relatively small manufacturer. The quality of its products did present opportunities for growth. But this was not the route it chose to travel.

This has changed since becoming a part of Echlin. We've succeeded in establishing the philosophy, based on our own experiences over so many years, that quality, once built into a product, can be maintained at the same high level regardless of expanded volume. In fact, the chances of even improving it are increased because of the greater tendency to adopt new technology that simultaneously refines and raises production.

So, there's a new slogan at Lipe—"Going for Growth."

And with an advanced new clutch especially designed for the original equipment truck market, the company definitely is on a growth course.

Revitalized Force

Graubremse's progress is something else I've followed with close interest, recalling the work I had the opportunity of doing with our predecessor subsidiary, Berg, when Beryl and I were in Heidelberg some years back.

Most of that work involved calling on Berg's present and prospective customers. In doing so, I was greatly impressed with the high caliber of people in the West German motor vehicle manufacturing industry, their attention to quality, and their products which have won them such a high standing throughout the world.

Hence, it's particularly satisfying, having done some of the groundwork that led to our acquiring the company, to see Graubremse growing as a vital and respected part of the European industry.

Here was a company that had been founded by one of the well-known automotive pioneers, August Grau, in 1927. Since that was but three years after Earl and I had taken over the Schnerr operation in San Francisco, I've had a natural affinity for the firm as one dating back to the early days.

Prior to its acquisition by Echlin in 1984, however, Graubremse had fallen on pretty hard times. Its manufacturing facilities had not kept pace with technological innovations and improvements. It had lost considerable status in the market, and was having a difficult time competing with other producers who had modernized and pursued more aggressive policies.

Yet, Fred's vision told him that it was a company which could be revitalized. And this has been done.

A great turnabout has been achieved with Echlin's infusion of capital, modernization of the plant in Heidelberg, building of a new plant in Regensburg, and introduction of a new program of research and development.

Today, Graubremse is a vital force in the European original equipment market and aftermarket. It has branches and service facilities in Belgium and Austria, as well as licensees in Spain and Yugoslavia. It has regained respect and acquired confidence.

Though the company is part of our Grau Girling joint venture in England, the two firms do not duplicate products. Graubremse manufactures a different type of air brake system from Grau Girling, and also produces hydraulic brake systems. At its new plant in Regensburg, the company specializes in draw bars, the links between trucks and trailers. With quality the key factor, these draw bars have 50 percent of the European market.

Graubremse will grow, we're sure. It is moving forward with existing products and developing new high-tech products. That it has regained and is extending its prominence is an accomplishment of which Echlin is proud to be a part.

The Human Equation

In this capsule review of Echlin's presence in Europe, much emphasis has been placed on the quality of our subsidiaries' manufacturing facilities and products.

People—dedicated, imaginative, talented, hard-working people—are fundamental to quality.

Although I personally have met and talked with only a few of our present European managers and technicians, this I know:

They are everything mentioned above.

This I know from things Fred has told our board about them, from Roger Storey's analyses, from reports the individual managers have made, and certainly from what is being achieved over there.

Fred has followed a wise policy. Rather than sending Echlin people to Europe to run the companies, he has left them in the hands of European managers. They know their own operations, the markets, the customers, and the European ways of doing business.

They have been encouraged to use their own initiative, to innovate, to go forward in directions their instincts tell them to go. And they have been given resources that enable them to do so.

The results speak for themselves. And there is every sign that we have only begun to see fulfillment of the great promise Europe holds for us, alongside of great things that still lie ahead for us here in America.

On this note, it's time to bring this story of Echlin and my participation in it for 73 exciting, rewarding years to a close. I leave it for a future company historian to record what I know will be a continuing story of growth, and most important of all, of contribution to the progress of this wonderful industry.